The Piccadilly
World of Golf
1972

*The Royal and Ancient clubhouse at St. Andrews
– the home of golf – pictured from the old stone
bridge which crosses the Swilcan Burn on the 18th
fairway.*

THE PICCADILLY WORLD OF GOLF

1972

Compiled and edited by

GOLF WORLD MAGAZINE

Contributors

Henry Longhurst
Pat Ward-Thomas
Ben Wright
Mark Wilson
Raymond Jacobs
George Houghton
John Jacobs
Herbert Warren Wind

WAYLAND PUBLISHERS LONDON

SBN 85340 235 3
Copyright © 1972 by
Golf World Magazine Limited and Wayland Publishers Limited
First published in 1972 by Wayland Publishers Limited,
101 Grays Inn Road, London, W.C.1

Printed by Jarrold and Sons Ltd, Norwich

Contents

21 Results Tables

I

The Piccadilly Story

George Hammond

It was in 1963 that the idea of the Piccadilly World Match-play Championship was conceived. No one present at that early meeting could have visualised the outstanding success which the tournament has become.

The concept was unique. It was to bring together eight of the best players in the world in 36-hole match-play.

Attention was next paid to the U.S.P.G.A. Championship and to the Individual Trophy of the Canada Cup matches, as well as to the Open Championships of Australia, New Zealand, South Africa and Canada. In any event, invitations were to be based on the competitor's achievements in the preceding year and on his general status in international golf. The field for the first Piccadilly Championship in 1964 emerged as the year unfolded. Arnold Palmer, who had earlier been invited on his record, and who had shown a positive interest in helping to launch the event, dramatically won his fourth U.S. Masters. When the field was being chosen it was clear that the U.S. Masters Champion, the United States and British Open Champions would be automatic choices as, of course, would be the holders of future Piccadilly World Match-play Championships.

So the stage was set and the West course at Wentworth, close to London and a tough test of golf, was chosen for the event. By early October it was geared to take the first World Match-play Championship.

The next Champion chosen was Ken Venturi, who after a long lean spell won the U.S. Open. The late Tony Lema took the British Open at St. Andrews at his first attempt, on his first visit to the Old Course. Gary Player (Australian Open Champion), Bruce Devlin (New Zealand Champion) and Jack Nicklaus (individual Canada Cup winner), joined the list. Neil Coles won the British Match-play Championship and Peter Butler, who had played with great distinction in the Masters, the Carling World Championship and the British Match-play – in which he was losing finalist – made up the exclusive group.

The man of this tournament, without any doubt, was Arnold Palmer. On many an occasion in his career he had risen to golfing heights and once again he pulled himself to the top at Wentworth. Palmer was drawn against Peter Butler. The match was cut and thrust throughout the 36 holes, at the end of which, having won one up, Palmer said of Butler: "He scared the hell out of me."

Gary Player won his first-round match

9

against Ken Venturi with an outstanding display of putting, and Tony Lema lost to Neil Coles. The last of the first-round matches brought together the younger generation in Jack Nicklaus and Bruce Devlin. In this match Devlin played with cool composure and won by 3 and 2. There was an incredible start to the Palmer versus Player semi-final match. Both men are very tough competitors. They are also very close friends, but this was set aside in a brilliant match in which Palmer reached the turn in 35 and found himself one down. However, he covered the next nine in 34 and due to the fact that Player's putting was troubling him, went in to lunch four up. Any hopes that Player may have had for recovery were rudely dashed by Palmer's start in the afternoon – eagle, par, birdie, birdie, birdie, birdie (3, 3, 3, 4, 2, 3). Poor Player could not stand this sort of pressure and eventually went down 8 and 6.

In the other semi-final Neil Coles beat Bruce Devlin in a dour but not dramatic match.

The final between Arnold Palmer and Neil Coles was interesting. One, a man whose bearing on a golf course could excite thousands of faithful followers, the other quiet, reserved, dedicated, but a tough and immensely difficult man to beat, particularly round the Wentworth West course.

It is always difficult to compare match-play figures with what might have happened in medal play, but suffice it to say that this memorable match produced some fantastic golf from both competitors. The morning round was cut and thrust all the way and Coles went to lunch two up. In the afternoon Palmer needed a four at the 36th hole for a score of 65. Considering that the course was playing long, and that there were thousands of spectators, this was truly a magnificent performance. Neil Coles can take consolation

from the fact that he was only beaten 2 and 1, for there are few golfers alive who would have lived with Arnold Palmer that day.

Because of the attraction of the play, the dignity of Arnold Palmer as Champion and the enthusiasm of the large galleries the seal was set on the first Piccadilly World Match-play Championship and was to prove a forerunner of things to come.

The concept of the 1965 event remained the same. Eight of the leading golfers in the world were to be invited on the basis of their championship achievements and on their overall status in world golf.

Arnold Palmer as defending Champion was automatically invited, Gary Player won the U.S. Open Championship, Kel Nagle, New Zealand Open Champion and runner-up to Gary Player in the U.S. Open was also invited. Peter Thomson won the British Open and Tony Lema won the Carling World Championship. They, together with Neil Coles, Christy O'Connor and Peter Alliss, made up the select field of one South African, two American, two Australian and three British players who had won collectively 10 British Open Championships, five U.S. Masters, five British Match-play titles and two U.S. Opens.

The semi-final line-up looked fascinating – defending Champion Palmer against Thomson, U.S. Open Champion Player against Lema.

Little did anyone realise that they were going to see some really great match-play golf and, in one case, probably the most spectacular match-play contest of all time.

A large crowd followed the first match and saw Thomson go ahead at the short second, a lead which he held until the 12th hole. He then won the 13th and 14th to go three up, but Palmer quickly retaliated by winning the 15th and 16th in birdies. To stop any sort of

Palmer charge, Thomson quickly won the 17th and 18th, also in birdies, and went to lunch four up. He also won the first hole in the afternoon round and was therefore in a very commanding position even against a man like Palmer, who won the seventh and eighth with birdies to reach the turn two down and then promptly lost the ninth and short 10th when he missed the green with his tee shot. He won the 11th, 12th and 13th when Thomson had a lapse of concentration on the greens, and they halved the short 14th in par three. In true Palmer style, which brought from the fans a crescendo of cheers and applause, he played the par-five, 480-yard 15th with a drive, four-iron and a six-yard putt to level the match. The atmosphere was electric and people were now awaiting the inevitable and famous "Arnie Charge", which has won him so many dramatic successes. But again the crowd had to wait. His drive at the 16th went on, it seemed, for ever. He then played a real duffer's shot – a wedge into the bunker short of the green. The best he could do was to get down in three more, and the Australian won the hole with a solid par four.

Thomson was now one up and there were only two holes left – two of the most dangerous and difficult holes in golf and because of their length, both par fives, more suited to Palmer's play than to Thomson's. Palmer hit two huge woods to the edge of the 17th and Thomson had to be content with two woods and a pitch. Palmer putted to within one yard and Thomson missed with his putt for his birdie. Everyone now waited for Palmer to sink his to halve the match, when horror of horrors, the putt never hit the hole. Thomson one up, one to play.

Palmer again hit two enormous woods to the 18th, but his second caught the right-hand bunker. Thomson again had to be

happy with two woods and a chip which he put eight feet from the pin. Palmer splashed out of the bunker to 12 feet and in true style sank the putt. Now Thomson had a difficult putt for victory. The ball hit the lip, spun round, and then just staggered into the hole. The crowd roared its approval to the end of a thrilling match which kept them all on their toes until the very last.

However, in the other semi-final between Gary Player and Tony Lema, being played half an hour behind, there were scenes of bewilderment and disbelief – a match that because of its incredible achievement in this standard of golf deserves a detailed explanation.

The first three holes were halved in par, and then at the long fourth Player's four-iron finished five yards short of the pin. He studied the putt for some considerable time and sure

enough it curled straight into the back of the hole. Thus he was one up, which he remained until the turn. Their respective medal scores would have been 34 for Player and 35 for Lema, against a par of 36. At the next hole Player hit a five-iron and finished eight feet from the hole. Lema hit the trees and finished in rough ground, but scrambled a shot on to the green about 20 feet past the hole and then made the putt. Player missed his and so the hole was halved. Player still one up.

Then an extraordinary thing happened. For the next eight holes Lema went 4, 4, 4, 2, 4, 3, 4, 4 – six birdies and 32 shots overall on the Burma Road's most difficult holes. Against this onslaught, except for the 11th, 12th and 13th which he played badly, the little South African played strict par and in fact holed a difficult putt for a birdie on the 18th. Nevertheless, he went to lunch six

On two separate occasions GARY PLAYER *has beaten Jack Nicklaus on the 14th green in the final of the Piccadilly World Match-play Championship.*

down then promptly lost the first hole of the afternoon to yet another birdie. Seven down with 17 to play. This was the end for Player – or so it seemed – but Player is not one to give up. He birdied the second and third holes to win both, halved the fourth with another birdie, sinking a critical, downhill putt, and promptly birdied the short fifth to win that. Four down with 13 to play. He then missed a short putt on the sixth to lose and halved the next three holes in determined golf. Five down with nine to play – an impossible task?

He won the short 10th with a par-three when Lema again missed the green, and then birdied the 11th to snatch that one as well. They halved the 12th in par and then Player hit two beautiful shots to the 13th finishing 10 feet from the pin. Lema had hooked his drive off the tee and all he could do was hit it a few yards down the fairway with his second.

He then played to the front edge about 30 feet from the pin and after great deliberation holed the monster. Player now had a nasty curling putt for yet another birdie and a win. In a tense atmosphere and in a cocoon of concentration the little man in black hit it straight into the back of the hole. The next two holes were halved in par and, with the strain now beginning to tell, Lema snap-hooked into the trees at the 16th and lost the hole. Player one down and two to play. The long 17th was halved in tight birdies, neither man giving an inch and so to the 18th tee.

Both hit good drives but Lema was short with his second to the green. Player then hit a shot with his four-wood the likes of which, he said afterwards, he had never played before. He hit it so hard that he nearly swung himself off his feet. The ball flew towards the green with slight draw, pitched on the right side and rolled to within 10 feet. Lema pitched up but could only make his par five, and Player,

knowing that he had two for a win, took both.

So this incredible match went to the 37th hole. Both players were now under considerable strain and in fact among the vast crowd which lined both sides from tee to green were unbelieving expressions. Player was on the green in two wonderful shots and Lema pulled his second into a bunker. Suffice it to say that he could not get down in two more – Player could!

So this fantastic match was over. Player nearly fainted and had to be helped back to the clubhouse and as for poor Lema – he was a man in a state of shock. Although these two great competitors had played in many harrowing and nerve-wracking tournaments, neither man had ever played in such a duel as this. One thing for certain: they would both go down in the history of the game as having participated in one of the greatest golf matches ever played.

And so the final. Could Thomson or Player really be able to bring their skills to bear once again. The morning round was played with quiet determination. All square after nine and Thomson one up at lunch, only one shot separating them. During the afternoon round Player applied some pressure with three birdies in the next nine holes to be two up after 27 holes. Thomson retaliated with an eagle at the 30th to be one down, but by now the strain was really telling. He missed the green at the 31st to lose that hole and again at the 32nd to lose both that and the match.

The field for the 1966 event was as strong as ever. Gary Player defending Champion, Arnold Palmer, Jack Nicklaus, winner of both U.S. Masters and British Open and Billy Casper U.S. Open Champion. Peter Thomson five times winner of the British Open and also British Match-play champion, Neil Coles, Robert de Vicenzo, and Dave Thomas made up the field.

The first semi-final between two old friends, Arnold Palmer and Gary Player, produced some marvellous golf. All square after nine holes. Palmer then birdied the 10th to go one up. They halved the next four holes, two of them in birdies. Then Player won the long 15th with a birdie to square the match. Tense duelling followed and they went to lunch all square.

The 12th hole was probably the one which cost Palmer the match. On the back of the green in two shots he watched Player pitch on 15 feet short of the pin for three. Palmer's approach putt was weak and then Player downed his for a four. Palmer then missed his next putt, and a hole he looked certain to win was lost.

He won the 15th when Player hooked into the woods and the 16th they halved in birdies. So Palmer was now dormy two down.

The 17th was an extraordinary hole for both players. Palmer drove first and hooked it just out of bounds. He then immediately drove another ball. Player then proceeded to hook his shot which just stayed in bounds. He backhanded it out on to the fairway when it was announced that a spectator had kicked his ball. He requested, and was given, a free drop. Arnold then hit a tremendous shot to the back of the green having now played four. Player played short and then pitched on for four. Palmer needing to win this hole to stay alive really concentrated on his putt which actually hit the hole. Player carefully took his two putts which halved the hole in six and won him the match 2 and 1.

The other semi-final also produced some sensational golf. Nicklaus playing the same golf as the previous day completely overwhelmed Billy Casper and was six up at lunch. Casper obviously felt that he still had a chance, however. He eagled the 19th, lost the 22nd and won the 23rd and 24th.

Nicklaus played the 26th and 27th badly and reached the turn only two up. He won the 11th when Casper three-putted to be three up, but the redoubtable Casper thrust back by birdieing the 14th and 16th. Nicklaus one up, two to play.

The long 17th hole, more suited to the power of Nicklaus produced the contrast of the two players. Nicklaus powered two enormous shots to the green and Casper played conservatively to rely on a pitch and a putt. Unfortunately he misjudged the chip and could not make the putt for his four. Nicklaus made no mistake with his two putts and so entered the final against Player.

The final between these two great players produced two things. Firstly, and one that tends to be obscured by the sensationalism of the second, was the quality of the play. Throughout Player played superb golf and Jack Nicklaus was the first to acknowledge this at the presentation. He beat Nicklaus by the margin of 6 and 4, which as anyone will realise is an achievement in itself when playing such an opponent.

The second feature of this match is known as the "Nicklaus–Duncan incident", and it is here that we take the match up.

Player was one up on the ninth tee and drove his ball straight down that fairway. Nicklaus pulled his drive into a ditch in the rough near the railway track. Referee Colonel A. A. Duncan allowed him to drop out of the ditch under penalty of one shot. As he lined up his shot, he claimed that a Piccadilly cigarette advertising sign obstructed his line to the green and as this was a temporary hazard asked the referee whether he could drop again without penalty to enable him a clear shot. Colonel Duncan said that he was not entitled to this relief as he considered there was a clear shot. Nicklaus hacked at the ball and remained in the rough. Player by

Left-handed New Zealander BOB CHARLES *beat Gene Littler for the title in 1969 at the 37th hole after one of the most devastating short-game and putting displays.*

this time had played his second to the green, and Nicklaus, after another smash at the ball, conceded the hole.

All might have remained calm, but following further discussion on the 10th green, Colonel Duncan withdrew and Gerald Micklem refereed the remainder of the match. This naturally caused an outburst of publicity which tended to swamp the rest of the play. Jack however birdied the 10th and 11th to square the match and once again the battle was on. Gary in true fashion counter-attacked and at the half-way was four up. He then continued the pressure and eventually won by the handsome margin of 6 and 4.

Player came back in 1967 to defend his title and was drawn against American Gay Brewer who had earlier that year won the U.S. Masters Championship. Their first-round encounter proved to be the longest in the short history of the event, victory going to Player in the gathering dusk on the 39th hole.

The first of the semi-finals between those old opponents Player and Thomson was to be an exciting match. Once again Player went to lunch three down. However, he squared the match with an eagle three at the 15th, but lost the 16th to a birdie from Thomson to go one down again. On the 17th Thomson drove down the middle, but Player going for the big one lashed it out of bounds. Three off the tee and another shot to the edge of green and two more putts were not good enough against Thomson's solid five. So the Australian avenged his defeat of 1965 when Player beat him in the final. The other semi-final between Palmer and Casper produced some great golf. At the end Palmer beat Casper by 3 and 2.

The final between Thomson and Palmer always looked as though it would be a good contest, and so it proved. After 18 holes the match was all square, both men going round in 70. After 27 holes they were still all square – when Palmer charged. Birdie, par, eagle, birdie to go three up. Thomson proved just what a tough competitor he is. He birdied the 14th, eagled the 15th and birdied the 16th. Of these he won only two because Palmer held him also with a birdie at 16. They halved the 17th in par, and when Thomson missed with his putt at the 18th he immediately walked over to congratulate Palmer.

So the first four Piccadilly World Match-play Championships had seen just two winners – Arnold Palmer and Gary Player.

The stage for the 1968 event was set and some new faces joined the select group. Lee Trevino, the laughing, joking American who won the 1968 U.S. Open at Oak Hill, Rochester, New York, his first major tournament win. This was his first appearance before galleries in the South of England. Next was Tony Jacklin, without doubt the brightest of any British golfer, chosen for his tremendous record in 1967 in British golf and also the first British golfer to win a tournament in America for many years – the Jacksonville Open. Third newcomer was Bob Charles of New Zealand, the great left-hander who had won many international titles including the British and Canadian Opens. Lastly Brian Huggett who won the British Match-play Championship and was no stranger to the rigours of the Burma Road, but he was to lose on the last green to Palmer in the opening match.

In the first semi-final Bob Charles playing steady golf beat a Palmer who had completely lost his touch. In the other semi-final Player was two up after 27 holes, but Jacklin in appalling conditions strung together six birdies in the next nine holes to square the match. It was now too dark to continue and the match was stopped until the next day, which was completely washed out by tor-

rential rain so they both had to wait another 24 hours before recommencing battle.

The Saturday morning broke clear. Player and Jacklin teed off and both hit the fairway. Jacklin played a lovely second to the front of the green, but Player pulled his below the left-hand bunker. He chipped up to within eight feet. Jacklin left his long putt four feet from the pin. In typical Player style, the little man hit his putt into the back of the hole. The pressure was on Jacklin, the putt missed the hole, so Gary Player went through to yet another Piccadilly final.

The final between left-hander Charles and Gary Player was another close contest. All square after nine holes they went to lunch with Player one up. In the afternoon they halved the first eight holes, when Charles then bogied the ninth to lose it. He won back the short 10th and the 11th, both with birdies and they then halved the next three holes. Player won the 15th with a birdie, and then hung on to the last hole with his lead of one up.

So Gary Player had now won the Piccadilly World Match-play Championship three times. A great record and one which won him the magnificent trophy outright.

The line-up for the 1969 event was interesting. Gary Player, defending Champion, played against Jean Garaialde of France, invited because of his sensational season on the European circuit. He won the Spanish, French, German and Swiss Opens. Unfortunately poor Jean came across a Gary Player who was utterly ruthless and in brilliant sunshine turned on a six-under-par performance to hand the Frenchman a 10 and 9 beating.

The second match was between two newcomers. Gene Littler, one of the most beautiful swingers in golf and Ray Floyd of America, who won the U.S.P.G.A. Championship.

Littler turned on the heat in the afternoon to win by 6 and 5.

Britain's Maurice Bembridge winner of the British Match-play Championship and Bob Charles made up the third match, but against tremendous figures he went down 6 and 5.

The last of the first day's matches was between Tony Jacklin, now holder of the British Open, and studious Tommy Aaron from America. Throughout, Jacklin's game was not up to his usual standard and from the first he always seemed to be struggling. In fact the morning round was more notable for its evenness than the quality of the golf. Jacklin took the lead for the first time at the 20th. He lost the next hole to a birdie – and from then on Aaron took command. From the 26th to the 32nd – seven holes, he scored 21 shots which annihilated Jacklin by 6 and 4.

So the semi-finals were between Gary Player and Gene Littler and Bob Charles and Tommy Aaron. Once again Wentworth weather took over, this time not rain but a heat mist, which delayed play for three hours.

Littler did not start well and was one down after four holes. After this his swing clicked and he shot seven consecutive threes at Player – par, birdie, birdie, birdie, birdie, par, birdie. Gary was now three down but, going for his fourth Piccadilly win, he sparked a tremendous comeback. He reduced the long 12th to an eagle three and he birdied the short 14th to reduce the deficit to one hole. He lost the 16th to yet another three by Littler, his eighth birdie in 11 holes. Stretching his incredible run of birdies to 10 in 13 holes, Littler reached the half-way stage in 65 shots to be two up.

They took only 15 minutes for lunch, and in the afternoon Littler gave him no chance to win by 4 and 3.

The other semi-final was remarkable for its sustained closeness of splendid scoring. Charles won the second and third, the fifth and the sixth were exchanged in birdies, and every other hole was halved in under par until Bob was bunkered at the 18th. This was his only five of the round which he completed in 66 to Aaron's 67.

The afternoon saw Charles at his best. Implacable concentration, and marvellous rhythm. It was sheer devastation and Aaron never had a chance. Charles reached the turn once again in 31 shots and when he got threes at the 10th and 11th it was all over – 9 and 7.

Bob Charles proved that he is not merely the best left-handed golfer, but one of the best golfers in the world today, with a superb exhibition of power and precision golf.

His triumph over Gene Littler in the final was a demonstration of magnificent iron play from the fairways, and some of the greatest putting seen in this country in a decade. Gene Littler said after the match: "Bob Charles is the greatest putter in the world today, including Billy Casper. He must have sunk more footage of putts today than in any other final in the history of golf."

Charles clinched the title at the 37th "sudden-death hole". The best shot of the day, a four-iron to within two feet of the pin, gave him a formality of a putt for an eagle three, but the one that he holed to save his neck at the 36th was 27 feet, an absolute miracle of concentration.

And so to the 1970 event. The tournament which by now was regarded as being one of the top five in the world has never failed to produce at least one memorable match and has provided all golfers with a splendid climax to the British tournament season.

This year saw one of the strongest fields ever assembled. Defending champion Bob

Charles, Tony Jacklin, the first British winner of the Open Championship for 18 years, and the first British winner of the American Open for 50 years. He was also the first golfer since Ben Hogan in 1953 to hold both titles within a span of 12 months. Billy Casper, winner of the U.S. Masters, Jack Nicklaus, winner of the British Open, Dave Stockton, winner of the U.S.P.G.A. Championship. Also playing were Gary Player, Australian Open Champion, Gene Littler 1969 finalist and Lee Trevino, top money-winner in America.

Jacklin avenged his earlier defeat by Player, Stockton beat Charles, Trevino won on the last green against Casper and Nicklaus finished Littler with an eagle three at the 35th.

So we had the clash of giants in the semi-final and a match which the world wanted to see. Nicklaus versus Jacklin – British Open

Champion against U.S. Open Champion. Super-star against the best British golfer. Ironically it was not this match that produced the golfing spectacle. Drama and excitement was reserved for the all-American semi-final between Dave Stockton and colourful Lee Trevino. Between them they blazed eight birdies and one eagle on the homeward nine holes, which put former U.S. Open Champion Trevino back in 32, ahead by four holes. In the afternoon he sprinted along and hardly missed a fairway to squash Stockton 7 and 6.

Try as he might Jacklin could not find his touch on the greens and as every golfer knows the insidious effect of this gradually eats into the rest of the game. Even the little flurry of interest when he went from five down to three down in the afternoon was illusory. All that happened was that Nicklaus failed to get a

By missing this putt TONY JACKLIN *lost at the first extra hole of his semi-final match against Player in 1968. Torrential rain caused a delay of 24 hours between completion of the first 36 holes and the playing of the one extra hole necessary to decide the match.*

couple of pars and Jacklin did not three-putt. The match ended by Nicklaus winning 5 and 4. Neither player had anything happy to say about their game.

So for the first time there was to be an all-American final. Trevino who without doubt had played the best golf throughout the week, and was really confident about his game, against Nicklaus who was certainly not. The match was one proof that Jack Nicklaus must be the best golfer today. From his previous poor performance the day before, he rose to the occasion against Lee Trevino to provide yet another astonishing final for this championship.

The golfers were in complete contrast. Nicklaus orthodox and deliberate about his whole game; Trevino quick and impulsive, pacing the greens like a tiger. Trevino dropped a shot at the 13th to go one down, and lost two more when Nicklaus birdied the 16th and 17th. So at lunch Trevino was round in 69 and three down to Nicklaus's 66.

Trevino eagled the first after lunch to get one back, but then bogied the short 23rd. Nicklaus again birdied the 25th and won the 26th when Trevino hit his shot far into the water. Both men birdied the 27th. Nicklaus, 32 shots, was now five up.

Nicklaus lost the short 28th when he missed the green and also the 29th when Trevino's birdie putt dropped in. Trevino then demonstrated remarkable shot-making qualities. He won the 31st when Nicklaus bogied and then nearly holed his tee shot at the short 32nd to win that as well. Trevino also won the 16th with a birdie three which brought him back to 1 down and 2 to play.

It was the 35th hole which provided the tragedy of the match. This long dog-leg, which so often in the past has ruined many a score, waited its chance again. Trevino, now only one down, rushed to the tee and played

the ball with a draw, hoping that it would bounce into the uphill side of the fairway and kick straight. He had played the hole this way before. This time, however, the ball did not kick straight but carried on out of bounds.

Nicklaus, determined not to make the same mistake choked down to an iron and with his solid par five it was all over.

Defending champion Nicklaus returned to Wentworth at the end of a disappointing 1971 season, having failed to win a major championship. He was opposed by Arnold Palmer, Gary Player, Tony Jacklin, Masters winner Charles Coody, Bob Charles, Neil Coles and diminutive Formosan Liang Huan Lu who had created such a sensation as runner-up to Lee Trevino in the Open Championship at Birkdale. But Trevino himself, without question the year's most successful player, honoured an earlier commitment and passed up a chance to add the Piccadilly World Match-play title to the Open Championships of America, Canada and Britain that he had captured in one golden month earlier in the year.

Biggest surprise of the first round was provided by "Mr. Lu's" short-hitting but accurate campaign against Nicklaus. He lost the first three holes, but had squared the match by lunchtime, finally going down by the unexpectedly narrow margin of 2 and 1. Coles disposed easily of Coody by 5 and 4, but a far from fit Jacklin – he had spent the previous day in bed with gastro-enteritis – could not take advantage of Player's lack of early form and duly lost by 4 and 3. The best match of the day was the Palmer–Charles cliff-hanger which Palmer sent into extra time with a 20-foot birdie putt at the 36th. But his initiative was short-lived, Charles finishing the match with a birdie four at the first sudden-death hole.

In the first semi-final Coles lost the first

two holes to Nicklaus, but recovered quickly to win the next three in a row. Nicklaus slowly regained the upper hand, finishing the round in 68 to be five up. A similar pattern emerged in the afternoon, Nicklaus winning three of the first four holes and then losing the next three, but he came back strongly for a 7 and 5 victory.

Player got off to an equally fast start in his afternoon round against Charles, winning the first three holes. It was just as well that he did, for Charles fought back in a scrappy match to lose by only 2 and 1.

Player and Nicklaus had met in the final in 1966, the South African concluding the proceedings on the 14th green with an impressive 6 and 4 victory, but in 1971 Player was constantly fighting a hook while Nicklaus improved with every round. The first 11 holes were halved with a display of precision golf before Nicklaus birdied the 12th and 13th to go two up. Player came back immediately, winning the 14th and 15th, where Nicklaus failed to hole from two feet for a half. This disastrous putting lapse caused Nicklaus to slightly alter his putting action and although he had lunched with a one-hole lead, he threw it away dramatically in the afternoon by missing short putts at three of the opening four holes. Player won all four holes and finished the match on the 14th green exactly as he had done five years before – but this time by a 5 and 4 margin.

In its eight years the Piccadilly World Match-play Championship has produced a marvellous parade of the most talented players in modern-day golf and matches of incomparable interest and drama.

There are nowadays very few tournaments which give world-class players the opportunity of man-to-man combat and the feeling of battle which so strongly involves the spectators in this, the ancient and original form of golf.

2

Match-play is Real Golf

Henry Longhurst

"Why aren't they televising this?" people very often say to me at match-play events. "Because," I reply – not that it is any business of mine anyway – "they would have to bring extremely expensive equipment (the most expensive coverage of any sport, so I believe) and, having covered the last five holes with cables stretching well over a mile and with about seven cameras, there would be no guarantee in match-play of seeing a single shot played." In other words all the matches may have finished by 6 and 5.

Even in international matches like the Walker and Curtis Cups, with foursomes in the morning, singles in the afternoon, you may still be caught out, or used to be in the past, before the days of video tape and instant playbacks and all the rest of it. In the 1959 Walker Cup match at Muirfield, for instance, when the promising young amateur Jack Nicklaus made his first appearance in this country, the top foursome went so fast (though you may hardly believe it) that they were already in the clubhouse when the transmission was due to come on and the second match was nowhere in sight. Today, of course, the first match would duly have been caught on video tape and replayed, a technique which has greatly added to the interest of broadcasts, especially early in the afternoon, which was always liable to be a barren time but can now be enlivened by showing the more exciting concluding stages of the morning's play. It is also responsible for the B.B.C. being able to present their entertaining "edited highlights" later on in the evening, since anything that goes on during the day, irrespective of its being transmitted or not, can to the discomfiture of elderly commentators who were hoping to be released to go back to the clubhouse and have a drink, be recorded for later use.

This means that "big" golf has become almost exclusively a stroke-play game, which it always was in America anyway. They did, it is true, for many years have a P.G.A. Match-play Championship, which lasted from 1916 to 1957 – won incidentally by Walter Hagen four years in a row from 1924, an almost incredible feat in 18-hole knock-out match-play, but television caught up with it in the end and they had to revert to stroke-play. An attempt a year or two ago to revive a knock-out tournament decided not by holes up and down but by the number of strokes taken was not reckoned a success as, from the television sponsorship point of view, they did not get the "right" pair in the final – any pair not including either Palmer or Nicklaus, or preferably both, not being "right" for television.

Around the turn of the century the

President of the U.S.G.A. was writing to a golf magazine urging American golfers to remember that golf was essentially a stroke-play game, and not to be influenced by the British idea of playing matches. Of course there is much logic in this, in that you go out to play 18 holes, so why should you not play all 18 and see how many you can do them in? There is also an awful logic in the inevitable fourballs, namely that you have gone out to play 18 holes, so why should you not finish every hole, counting your score, regardless of how your partner is doing? This is, of course, the main reason why four indifferent country club players, all counting their score, take five and a half hours to go round.

Nevertheless, I was brought up on the basis that, when we set out to play golf, either I play a match against you, or you and I play a match against him and him, or, if there are three of us, which is perhaps the best game of all since every stroke counts double, we each play against the other two. One of the nicest fellows in all golf must surely have been Freddie Tait, who won the Amateur in 1896 and 1898, only to be killed in the Boer War. You will see his picture, with his Black Watch sash across his chest, hanging in golf clubs all over the world and every time I look at it I think what a marvellous fellow he must have been. At any rate I go along with Freddie Tait when he

JACK NICKLAUS (left) *and* LEE TREVINO *were involved in a heavyweight knock-out contest in the 18-hole play-off to decide the U.S. Open Championship of 1971. This type of confrontation is golf at its best, maintains Henry Longhurst.*

said: "Match-play's the thing. Stroke-play is no better than rifle shooting."

Playing against a live opponent requires qualities quite different from, and in my opinion much superior to, those needed for stroke-play, for which one only needs to be able to wrap oneself up in a cocoon of concentration. If your playing partner's shot

in stroke-play bounces out of a tree and on to the green, you are quite pleased on his behalf. If he does the same thing in a match, it is difficult not to start gnashing your teeth and complaining that you have been robbed and furthermore – a fatal mistake – thinking how you are going to tell everyone about it when you get in.

All this, I think, is why the Piccadilly Match-play Championship is such a great tournament and, so far as I can judge, induces a greater sense of excitement than anything except perhaps the closing stages of the Open. You are not watching Nicklaus going round with Player: you are watching Nicklaus trying to knock Player out. In the

play-off for last year's U.S. Open at Merion between Nicklaus and Trevino the whole thing came suddenly to life – although play-offs are the most infernal nuisance to everyone concerned and should forthwith be abolished by "sudden death" (by which in any case the play-off itself will be decided, should it end in another tie). Here at last was no longer what Bernard Darwin called "one of these round and round and round again" tournaments but a real heavyweight knock-out contest between indisputably the two greatest players in the world at that moment. They traded blow for blow, holing putts at each other from all over the place, especially at the end, and it was an occasion I shall never forget.

Who, again, can ever forget that match when Player at Wentworth was seven down with 17 to play against Tony Lema and politely rebuked a spectator whom he overheard saying it was no good following this match any longer. The last six holes were seen by a vast audience on television and everyone who had ever suffered a landslide in match-play golf will have sympathised with Lema as the holes slipped remorselessly away. They will have known that awful feeling when you cannot see any possible way of ever halving a hole again, let alone winning one. Long may the flag of match-play flourish, say I. Down with rifle shooting!

A classic match-play encounter occurred during the Piccadilly World Match-play Championship when GARY PLAYER *was seven down to the late* TONY LEMA (left). *Player fought his way back to victory.*

JACK NICKLAUS *(also on previous page) and* ARNOLD PALMER, *the two most exciting tournament professionals of modern golf. Palmer dominated the game in the early 1960s – a position which Nicklaus took over in the second half of the decade. In 1972 Nicklaus won the first two legs of the modern Grand Slam – the U.S. Masters and U.S. Open, failing by one shot to add the British Open to his list.*

In an incredible month in 1971 LEE TREVINO
*won the Open Championships of America, Canada
and Britain. He discharged himself from
hospital to play in the American Open this year,
lost his Canadian title, but retained his British
crown with an impressive victory over* JACK
NICKLAUS *and* TONY JACKLIN *at Muirfield.*

TONY JACKLIN *brought British golf back to life when he became the first home player to win the Open Championship for 18 years at Lytham in 1969. He followed this fantastic success within a year with a seven-shot victory in the American Open in difficult conditions. He is the man largely responsible for the revival of British golf in the past three seasons.*

GARY PLAYER, *a physical fitness fanatic and South Africa's most successful golfer. Winner of all four Grand Slam events.*

3 Finding the Clubs to suit your Game

There are golf clubs, and golf clubs – and although racks of shining new mathematical masterpieces may attract you into a buying spree, how do you know they'll suit you?

You don't go into a shoe shop and ask for "that one on the right of the window, sort of brown colour, size nine, please", see them wrapped, pay and walk out.

You sit down. You try one on. And if you do not feel comfortable with it, or its mate, you hunt around until you find a pair that suit.

It's the same with golf clubs. What may well suit the club champion, or your next-door neighbour, could prove an absolute disaster for you.

Not that there is anything wrong with the material, or the manufacture, it's just a question of feel, balance and weight. So shop around.

Remember, once you have bought a set of clubs – and they can be costly – you are not likely to get them altered or exchanged. They are yours for good, or until such time as you decide to make another change. If you strive to make the best of what proves, for you, to be a bad set, your game is going to suffer. So you sell at a loss, and try again.

Far better to be patient and judicious in the first instance.

Forget any ideas you may have had about "trying out" clubs. No club professional, the "retailer", is going to allow you to walk around with a completely new set of clubs.

Many enlightened club professionals now

provide several clubs for trial purposes – allowing potential customers to try before they buy. But no professional can afford to stock a full range of trial clubs, so the greater your own knowledge of golf-club design and manufacture the better able you will be to narrow down the field before consulting your club professional for a final "fitting".

Within reason most golfers can improve or more fully enjoy playing, simply by using clubs that fit their style, strength, build and playing characteristics, so the opportunity of browsing in a shop armed with a little knowledge, is time well spent.

What do you look for?

Start with the grip. This must be the right size and in the right material. It is your only contact with the club and if uncomfortable with it, your shots are bound to suffer. See that it fits your hands. Thin grips for small hands, built-up grips for large hands, but experiment until you are satisfied.

Appearance and "feel" are important, although here it is a matter of personal preference.

If you have already consulted your club professional he will be able to tell you whether you are a player needing strong clubs, ideal for the powerful hitter, or clubs giving as much help as possible to the man less well physically equipped for the game.

Although the standard shaft lengths suit the majority of people there are exceptions, but here again consult your pro. Broadly speaking no one under 6 feet 2 inches needs lengthened clubs, but the very short, 5 feet 4 inches or less, should use shorter clubs.

Weight is important, and in general most golfers use clubs which are too heavy. Consult the table shown here – and discuss your own particular needs with a professional who has seen you play.

Finally, having obtained the ideal set of clubs, keep them in good condition. Clean the heads, use head covers, wash rubber grips with detergents, or treat leather grips sparingly with castor oil. It will save money – and improve your game.

A quick guide to norn

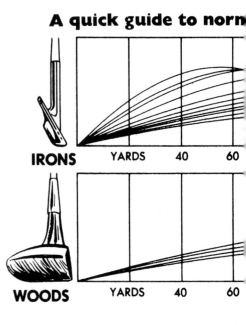

IRONS   YARDS   40   60

WOODS   YARDS   40   60

GUIDE TO CLUB SELECTION

TYPE OF GOLFER	SHAFT		SWING-WEIGHT	
	Men	Ladies	Men	Ladies
Powerful Fast swinger, hard-hitter Lively hand action	S (or even X)	R	D4-D7	D0-D3
Well-built, athletic Fast swinger, aggressive striker Good hand action	S	R or A	D2-D5	C9-D1
Average build Medium-pace swing, good club control Fair hand action, the " swinging-hit " player	R	A or L	D0-D3	C7-D0
Basically sedentary life Easy swing, lacks distance Sluggish hand-action	A	L	C9-D1	C6-C9
Slight or slender Getting on in years, movement restricted Slow swing, badly lacks clubhead speed, short of distance	A or L	L	C7-D0	C5-C8

Shaft key: X = extra stiff; S = stiff; R = regular; A = flexible; L = ladies

tances for low handicap players

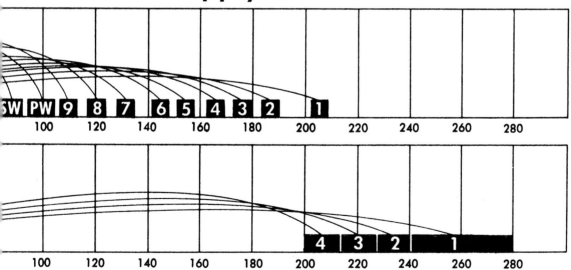

35

4 The British Comeback

Mark Wilson

When Britain's golf professionals returned home from the last world war, they still had in their minds that page of the military manual which encourages an army to march at the pace of the slowest man for safety. It may have proved a good tactic for the infantry, but it was a way of thinking that chained the feet of the Professional Golfers' Association for years.

Peace brought tremendous opportunities in a country starved of sport, and professional golf allowed so many of them to pass by while clinging to policies based on caution rather than new-era enterprise. The curb on leading amateurs joining the paid ranks to compete for tournament prize-money was the worst of all.

Eric Brown, who was to become a Ryder Cup player and team captain, suffered cruelly by it, and so did the game as a whole as some elder statesmen inside the P.G.A. seemed bent on making young amateurs pay dearly for the sins of those fathers who had once slammed clubhouse doors in their faces. In 1946 Eric Brown was shovelling coal as a railway fireman, and he used his summer holiday week to win the Scottish Amateur Championship title. Two months later he turned professional.

In the light of the rapturous reception top amateurs like Peter Oosterhuis and Bernard Gallacher now receive on entering the professional game, Brown's welcome was unbelievably cold.

It was five long years before he was allowed to win P.G.A. money. "They really made it difficult for a top amateur to turn

ERIC BROWN *had to serve a five-year apprentice-ship before he was allowed to win money in professional events in Britain. It was this iniquitous rule which held back the standard of British professional golf in the post-war years.*

professional in those days," he now recalls. "Anybody coming into the pro ranks as an assistant could play the tournaments after three years. If they took a full pro's job it was five. I went across and played the Continental championships, and, of course, a lot of local events in Scotland. I made a fair amount of money, enough to keep going."

So Brown braved and survived, but it was a narrow-minded system that cost professional golf a host of potential recruits who might have done much to avoid a Dark Age in which Britain failed to produce an Open champion for 18 years. "In Scotland alone we had a bunch of fellows," says Brown, "who were up to Walker Cup standard but were never considered because they couldn't afford to play in the show-pieces down south. Now they turn pro and start earning after six months, but in those days it was completely out for them because they couldn't take three years of getting something like £3 a week as an assistant."

While British golf stood still, the Americans were running ahead. It seemed at one time that a youngster had only to show promise in a junior State tournament to have a college scholarship for a prize. And as for champions, well, the United States P.G.A. looked upon it as a slight if they remained amateur. "Come and join us," was the offer, and players like Arnold Palmer, Gene Littler, Billy Casper and Jack Nicklaus took it up.

The gap between the two attitudes was reflected in prize-money totals for the British P.G.A. tournament circuit. In 1946 the official kitty was £20,785 and 10 years later it had grown to £25,440. A growth rate of just £534 a year!

By now five successive Open championships had fallen to overseas challengers, and it was obvious they were on a winning streak that still had a long way to go. Then, as unexpected as it was needed, came the moment that not only saved the pride of British golf but pointed the way to its new future. The comeback was about to start.

In the October of 1957, Dai Rees took the Ryder Cup team to Lindrick and whipped the Americans. It couldn't happen, but it did. I was there, along with 20,000 more, pinching myself to make sure it was real. The Americans had excuses, of course. The squad given Jackie Burke wasn't the best they could have put out. Funny though, there was no talk like that after they had taken a 3–1 foursomes lead on the first day. It all followed their 5–1 hammering in the singles, started by Eric Brown lighting the swift-burning fuse of Tommy Bolt's temper with a 4 and 3 defeat.

The momentum of that tremendous victory, the feeling that we could still do it, carried British golf into the 1960s and a complete new phase of planning. It was to be an exciting decade, paving the way for even more ambitious moves in the seventies with the capture of John Jacobs as P.G.A. tournament supremo and a £500,000 prize-money target.

As a first step the P.G.A. leaders held out a welcoming hand to top amateurs, eventually cutting down their "waiting period" to six months. And in they came, Guy Wolstenholme and Doug Sewell leading the way from the Walker Cup ranks. Ronnie Shade followed along with Peter Townsend, Clive Clark, enough to make up a whole international team. It served as a multi-purpose injection.

The publicity involved attracted the attention of new sponsors. Up soared the prize-money, £43,215 in 1959, then £177,755 only seven years later. Professional golf was now big business. Top amateur recruits established a new breed of full-time globe-

Successful international amateurs, like GUY WOLSTENHOLME *and* PETER OOSTERHUIS (above) *were given every encouragement to join the professional ranks in strict contrast to the treatment Eric Brown received in his early days.*

trotting tournament players. The incentive to work was there and the whole standard of the circuit gradually rose as part of the snowballing process.

Assistants coming on the tour soon got the message that the money was now there if they were good enough and determined. A lot came and went; one who stayed was Tony Jacklin. When he was a thin-faced boy at Potters Bar he holed a wicked putt on the last green to relieve me of a pound note. "What are you going to do now?" I asked, thinking about taking him to lunch. "Win the Open," he answered. He did, too. And the U.S. Open.

Now the P.G.A. was no longer marching at the pace of the slowest man. Everyone wanted to keep up with the fast-moving Jacklin. He has yet to be caught, but golf has prospered in every way as a result of the chase.

Progress has its problems, of course. In the mid-1960s assistants were pouring on to the circuit like so many Dick Whittingtons believing that the fairways were paved with gold. They threatened the image of the P.G.A. with their pre-qualifying rounds in the 90s, and something needed to be done. So a move was started to limit assistants to junior events until they had proved themselves by their performances.

It led to a resolution at an annual P.G.A. meeting, and just as it seemed the members were ready for a vote of acceptance, Henry Cotton stood up. He delivered an impassioned speech, pleaded "Let 'em all come" and won the day. And come they did, in their hundreds.

Inevitably there arrived the time when the long-sought and much-needed quality faced the threat of being swamped by quantity. Youngsters wouldn't accept that they were wasting their own time and that of everyone else. It was a hard world they thought should be softened: like by giving the winners less money and sharing more out among those at the bottom. A good way of sponsoring mediocrity. It persisted throughout the sixties and then, after one more abortive effort when a special general meeting failed to gain a quorum, the P.G.A. Executive Committee finally won. The normal assistant is now kept off the tour for two years unless his achievements in minor tournaments merit a waiving of the rule.

Along with the new young stars of the game came a crop of fresh leaders with way-out ideas. Geoffrey Cotton, a club professional, was one who began to pass "let's go the whole way" thoughts round the Executive table. The result was the most controversial piece of P.G.A. legislation yet – the introduction of the 1·68-inch big ball.

The arguments are too well known to need detailing again. But they set professional against professional as the extra six-hundredths of an inch destroyed the careers of some and made others the fine strikers they might never have been otherwise. All will be eventually settled, it is to be presumed, with the whole golf world adopting a uniform-sized ball. What will never be agreed by all, however, is the measure of influence the big ball has had on the professional game in Britain.

It was adopted by the P.G.A. in the belief that it could make our professionals better players. Is it coincidence then, its critics are now asked, that since its compulsory introduction the overseas domination of the Open has been broken, the Americans have been held to a Ryder Cup tie at Royal Birkdale, and given their hardest match ever in the States?

I am sure that the rising standard of British golf owes much to the big ball – but there will

JOHN JACOBS, *new tournament supremo who has secured sponsorship to the tune of more than half a million pounds for the 1972 circuit.*

The British Comeback

always be those windswept days when a sorry-looking tournament scoreboard casts serious doubts on its all-round suitability. Eric Brown, never one to mince his words, campaigned long and loud against it. Now, reflecting on the game's progress in recent years, he says: "Personally I don't think the big ball has made a damn bit of difference.

"Good players will be good players no matter what ball they play. The idea of the big ball making you a better player is absolute rubbish. No, the standard has risen because the top amateurs were let in and stiffer competition makes players work harder and take the game far more seriously than used to be done in the old days. Some of the big boys then used to step on the tee cold half the time, no practice. Mind you I wasn't one, I was a young buck in those days.

"I think, too, it is a matter of expenses being so high nowadays that to make ends meet you have to play well. Then there is the weight of numbers. Up to about 1957 there might be around 100 players in a tournament. Now we have anything up to 300, sometimes more, entering. Well, fair enough. There cannot be room for everybody so you cannot afford to miss a shot these days. This is the big answer to it – expenses against the prize money.

"The incentives are there and there is no reason why British golf shouldn't keep getting better. We have a lot of good youngsters coming up and John Jacobs is giving us all the opportunities. I am extremely happy about the future for I can only see British golf getting better and better."

After setting off at a slow pace, the professional game has marched a long way and Michael Bonallack was the first to hand it credit for the encouragement it has given all golf after leading Britain's amateurs to that 1971 Walker Cup victory awaited 33 years.

5 Jacklin's Swing Sequence

TONY JACKLIN sets up to the ball with a fairway wood with a slightly open position of feet, hips and shoulders. The lower half of the body is firmly set, already resisting

the turn of the upper body in the backswing. At the top of
the backswing the hips have turned through less than 45
degrees while the shoulders have made a 90-degree pivot.

Nearing impact position Jacklin slides his hips laterally to the left and also turns them anticlockwise out of the way to allow room for a powerful and free downward

and through blow with the arms and hands, bringing the club-head into the ball from inside the line through the ball to the target. Perfect co-ordination gives maximum power

On the professional tour Jacklin once swung the club on a much flatter, round-the-body plane. He now gets the club in a more upright position at the top of the swing,

clears the left side well in the downswing and hits through along the target line with a free-wheeling motion carrying hands and club-head to a high end-of-swing position.

48

6 The Modern Grand Slam

Ben Wright

ARNOLD PALMER *brought the Open Championship back to life. His attempts to win the waning British title (he was successful in 1961 and 1962) had crowds like this running riot over the course at Old Troon.*

If readers' letters are anything to go by there is still some confusion about exactly which four events constitute the modern era Grand Slam. Those with longer, fond memories of the late Bobby Jones are unable, or perhaps unwilling, to accept that the British and American Amateur Championships are no longer included among the "big four" events. The latter quartet, embracing the U.S. and British Opens, the U.S. Masters and the U.S.P.G.A. Championship came into being some time in the 1960s, when the magical presence of Arnold Palmer, Jack Nicklaus and an ever increasing company of world-class golfers gave back the British Open the prestige that had ebbed away in the previous decade. Needless to say the modern Grand Slam – winning all four championships in a single season – has yet to be achieved, although at the time of writing I am not alone in fancying Nicklaus to pull off this,

49

the greatest available triumph in the game, in the current season.

The British Open had perhaps reached its lowest ebb in 1959 after the great Bobby Locke had been sidelined by a car accident that damaged an eye – depriving the truly world-class South African of his impeccable short-game judgment when he was at the height of his powers. His then young and comparatively inexperienced countryman Gary Player was able to run up a six at the last hole of the Championship at Muirfield (two over par), shed his tears at the recorder's hut, having apparently thrown away the title, only to return to claim the trophy two hours later as the challenges of a much travelled club professional Fred Bullock (his daughter pulled his trolley) and the veteran Belgian Flory van Donck, aged 47, had duly melted away.

Since an obvious non-winner Syd Scott finished next – aged 46 – Sam King, 48, John Panton, 42 and the amateur Reid Jack tied with Christy O'Connor for fifth place, and 46-year-old Dai Rees was a further stroke behind, the 23-year-old Player hardly had to hold off a world-class field. But Lee Trevino undoubtedly did just that at Royal Birkdale in 1971, and the champion of 1972 was certain – at the time of writing – to have emerged at Muirfield from the best-ever field in a British Open.

Of the four events that constitute the modern Grand Slam, the organisation of the British Open has made by far and away the most progress since this mythical title was reborn. Jones had won the old version of the Slam in 1930 on the only occasion such a momentous feat was achieved – by winning the Open and Amateur Championships of both his native America and Britain. When Nicklaus turned professional in 1961 any chance of Jones's extraordinary triumph

being repeated, at least in the foreseeable future, was removed. Nowadays the majority of amateurs have neither the means to retain their status, nor the will-power to resist the lure of immense fame and fortune readily available on the professional tours on either side of the Atlantic. Nor, for that matter, has anyone emerged since Nicklaus boasting anything near the talent of big Jack or Jones in the last decade.

So it was that at the Centenary British Open of 1960 at St. Andrews, Palmer first appeared over here, shortly followed by Nicklaus at Troon in 1962 – with spectacular lack of success similar to that of the youthful Jones – and the Championship started to reacquire the status of a world-class event. Let no one underestimate the debt we owe to Palmer and Nicklaus in this respect. In order of preference and importance amongst the top-ranking players the British Open still ranks third of four to the U.S. Open and Masters tournament but is, in my opinion, now the equal of, if not superior even to the latter from the promotional angle of expertise and flair, and streets ahead of the U.S. Open.

The U.S.P.G.A. Championship is still the poor relation in the family quartet, largely because for years the policy of the U.S.P.G.A. in hawking around their premier event to the highest bidder caused it to be staged on what can kindly be referred to in American parlance as "Mickey Mouse" courses, or in British jargon "dirt tracks". Happily in recent years the U.S.P.G.A. has awakened to the importance of staging the traditionally last-played event of the Grand Slam at golf courses worthy of the name.

The National Cash Register Company's course in Dayton, Ohio, provided a very adequate test in 1969 – and was the scene of perhaps the ugliest race riot so far to have taken place on a golf course aimed at the

ROBERTO DE VICENZO, *winner of the Open Championship in 1967, threw away the chance of a play-off for the American Masters in 1968 when he signed an incorrect score-card. Immediate steps were taken to ensure privacy for players checking their cards at Augusta in the years that followed.*

South African Player, as he challenged the eventual winner Ray Floyd. The 1970 Championship was played at Southern Hills Country Club in baking hot Tulsa, Oklahoma, a marvellous golf course beloved of Ben Hogan, where the organisation, master-minded by the now regular U.S.P.G.A. Championship promoter Ed Carter, matched anything I have yet seen, even at Augusta or at the British Open. This was largely due to the enthusiasm and hospitality of the local people. For instance the lady courtesy car drivers would start work at five o'clock in the morning, and think nothing of turning out close to midnight to drive home guests from dinner parties. I now firmly believe I saw Hogan make his last public appearance on the course before the event, and it was not a pretty sight. Hogan's ailing knee – his left is strengthened by a steel brace – caused him to try to play every shot off the back foot. When his golf ball was situated below the level of his feet he was beaten before he started his backswing. After losing five dollars to Tony Jacklin, Hogan sat pensively over a snack lunch before scratching from the Championship and immediately returning home to Fort Worth. But he played one unforgettable golf shot born of anger and frustration at the 13th hole that day. After skying his drive Hogan let loose a two-iron shot that never left the flag and settled down six feet behind the hole some 230 yards away. Needless to say the great man missed the putt.

Last year's venue, P.G.A. headquarters at Palm Beach Gardens, Florida, provided a test of golf that puts a greater premium on brute strength than I think is justifiable, making Nicklaus an almost certain winner before the event started – and he duly obliged. But this is certainly preferable to

staging such an important championship at an inferior venue that produces a wedge-play and putting competition. This year's U.S.P.G.A. title will not easily be won either, since the Oakland Hills Club in Birmingham, Michigan, is one of the best known and toughest tests of golf favoured by the U.S.G.A. for the Open. Hogan and Gene Littler are among the famous names to have won the latter title there, while Walter Burkemo won the P.G.A. Championship at Oakland Hills in 1953 when the event was decided by match-play.

The U.S. Masters tournament at Augusta National Golf Club, Georgia, in April is traditionally the first of the four major titles to be contested – although Dave Stockton, winner of the 1970 P.G.A. title in Tulsa in August held the honour for only six months because the 1971 Championship was played, for once, in February. The brainchild of Jones and the present tournament director, or should I say dictator, Clifford Roberts, the Masters has acquired enormous stature and prestige in its comparatively short history. Launched in 1934, it is by far the youngest of the events that make up the Slam, and is, to all intents and purposes still a private club's invitational event. Many of the American professionals would like to change all that and make it another run-of-the-mill event as is the U.S.P.G.A., but thankfully they are unlikely to get their way. And contrary to all the snide stories trotted out annually with monotonous regularity, a Negro will play at Augusta as soon as he proves himself good enough by qualifying for an invitation.

Much of the immense reputation won by the Masters has been due to its incomparable setting in a former shrub nursery. When the tournament is played, thousands of azalea, redbud, red and white dogwood and mag-

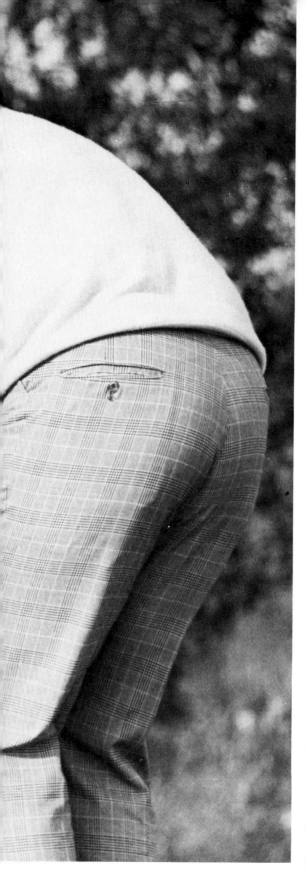

Since Bobby Jones won the original Grand Slam – British and American Amateur and Open Championships in 1930 – only JACK NICKLAUS *has emerged with the talent to take the four titles which make up the modern Grand Slam – British and American Opens, U.S. Masters and P.G.A. Championship.*

nolia bushes and trees are usually in delicate, glorious bloom. The course is closed for nearly half the year to ensure that it is brought lovingly to peak condition in April. If the grass becomes worn by thousands of hustling feet it is promptly dyed green in the early morning, and the murky brown lakes are tinted a deep blue for the benefit of colour telecasts. The backdrop of giant pines, hundreds of them more than 100 feet high make the scene possibly the most beautiful golfing panorama in the entire world. The clubhouse, a rambling old colonial building of infinite internal charm is painted a peerless white with dark green shutters, the latter being also the colour of all the concession stands, grandstands, television towers and the like that are carefully blended into the scenery to become as unobtrusive as possible.

It is the very permanence of the tournament's venue, and the ability of the myriad committees to concentrate with unparalleled zeal from year to year on improving their own facet of the operation that causes the Masters to be so superbly run, and such a wonderful showpiece. The tiniest detail is seldom overlooked, although it was a blind spot in this respect that indirectly led to the notoriously careless Roberto de Vicenzo's score-card fiasco in 1968. The Argentinian, never one for wasting time checking his score-card, botched his arithmetic and lost the chance of a play-off against luckless Bob Goalby. But there is no doubt that the lovable de Vicenzo had little chance to concentrate in the frenetic atmosphere and among thousands of milling fans engulfing him behind the 18th green. Needless to say the appropriate committee at Augusta saw to it that the players were hustled into a roped-off area and sat down in a tent thereafter.

The Masters is generally regarded by the players as the easiest of the four major titles

The Modern Grand Slam

When GARY PLAYER *won the Open Championship at Muirfield in 1959 he did so from a purely domestic field of club professionals.* ARNOLD PALMER's *insistence that the British title should be regarded as a world-class event brought the Championship back to life in the 1960s.*

to win. They base this supposition on the evidence that there are many substandard performers invited – some of them amateurs – many of them former champions included in the party for old time's sake. This is doubtless true – and in my opinion praiseworthy in a game growing ever less regardful for sentiment and tradition – but the atmosphere down the stretch at Augusta is still powerfully claustrophobic and nerve-shattering.

There is little doubt that the U.S. Open is the most difficult to win of the four. The entry is so enormous – 4,252 in 1972 – that an inferior player could not possibly hope to survive the local, regional and final qualifying tests. The British entry, which at the time of writing appeared likely to be well above the previous record and possibly in excess of 600, is tiny by comparison. The extraordinary fact that emerges from comparison of the two figures is that the British Open attracts entries from 27 different nationalities against the American Open's seven.

This is hardly surprising, since the British event is staged so magnificently by the Royal and Ancient Golf Club of St. Andrews, ably marshalled by their ebullient secretary Keith Mackenzie. The latter has done a remarkable globe-trotting job to literally sell the British Open wherever he goes with a sheaf of entry forms, and he was particularly delighted with the high number of Asiatic entries for this year's Championship. Just as it does at Augusta, the organisation of the British Open improves with each successive year, and the R. and A. have far greater problems in this respect.

They have no permanent venue, although the rota of Open Championship courses is a small one, getting smaller. They have – generally speaking – far less room in which to manœuvre with their tented villages and

the like, and the weather is an unknown, and often violent quantity at the links courses always used to house the British Open. It is therefore a notable triumph that the Masters tournament organisers saw fit to incorporate some of the more sophisticated scoring features found to be so efficient at the British showpiece. In return Mackenzie will be using some of the devices he discovered at Augusta this spring, when the Championship is staged at Muirfield in July – three weeks after its American counterpart.

When one has acknowledged that the U.S. Open is the premier event in the world there is little else to say in its favour. The United States Golf Association, in their slavish devotion to tradition at all costs – regardless of the need for progress – have slipped very far behind the R. and A. in their organisation. It seems utterly laughable that an organisation that reeks so headily of real tradition as does the R. and A. should be so willing to blow along with the winds of change, whereas the U.S.G.A. obstinately refuse to erect grandstands, or make their showpiece just that. The public seem to be almost disregarded as the United States officials run a Championship apparently for their own delight and enjoyment. One can only hope that they will eventually learn from the example set so perfectly by those in Augusta's corridors of power, and latterly adopted with outstanding success by the previously hidebound Royal and Ancient. Until they do so the Masters and British Open appear certain to remain far in front in the field of public entertainment, with the U.S.P.G.A. Championship gaining stature with impressive rapidity.

7 Ben Hogan - the Greatest Ever?
Pat Ward-Thomas

In any discussion as to the greatest golfer of the past half-century the names of Bob Jones, Ben Hogan and Jack Nicklaus stand alone. To attempt comparison between them, absorbing though it may be, is a purely academic exercise because far too many variables are involved. No man can do more than achieve indisputable supremacy in his own time, and thereby acquire an aura reserved only for those who do something better than anyone else in the world. However familiar as persons these supreme beings may become they quicken feelings far surpassing normal admiration for great skill, feelings of awe, even wonder, that they are not as other men. Never was this feeling more intense than when one was with Hogan.

There was a rare sense of the unforgettable about him, not simply because of his matchless skill but because of the force of his personality, a force more compelling in its fashion than the charm of Arnold Palmer, the ebullience of Lee Trevino or the amiable strength of Jack Nicklaus. There was about Hogan in his competitive years, as of no one else, an almost overwhelming sense of a man apart.

Within seconds of meeting him for the first time anyone would be aware that he was in the presence of a most unusual man, even without knowing of his eminence as a golfer. The outlines of his face, indelibly tanned by thousands of days in the sun, are unmistakably powerful, even cruel when the wide mouth is drawn down in concentration; the piercingly direct gaze could be cold as a winter dawn, and his economy of speech fearsome. In the tradition of the Far West Hogan does not believe in wasting words.

Even in a longish conversation I have never heard Hogan waffle; his replies to questions were invariably direct, sometimes alarmingly so; where a monosyllable would

Hogan's backswing was compact and flatter than the classical concept – but there was a wonderful sense of precision about his swing.

suffice he saw no reason to cloak it in useless verbiage. I recall waiting outside an airport for transport to a course some years ago; Hogan and his wife, Valerie, were there and eventually a bustling official approached and asked Hogan if he would care to ride down with Mr. Snead. Hogan looked straight at him and said quietly, "Not particularly." Not another syllable did he utter and the little man scarcely knew where to look. The Hogans rode alone.

The American Press as a whole are not famous for their deep insight into golf or for watching it and the players can be asked stupid questions. On one such occasion Hogan is said to have remarked that, "One day a deaf mute will win a tournament and no one will know what happened." Another time I was talking with him when a man approached and said, "I suppose you come to Augusta now to see your friends," – a lethal misunderstanding. Hogan chilled him with a glance and replied, "I see my friends in Fort Worth." On the other hand, if Hogan knew that a writer was genuinely interested, and watched the golf, he would take pains to explain the shot.

Tournament golf was not a social occasion for Hogan. He would enjoy chatting and having a drink with old cronies in the locker room, but even in the later mellower years one would never see him pausing here and there about the clubhouse or its precincts. It was as if he had need of no one, either on the course or off it, except for his wife; he seemed a man alone and I imagine sometimes a lonely man.

This very self-sufficiency indicated the force of character that had enabled him to endure and overcome privation and adversity, the like of which none of his great contemporaries have known. As a child he sold newspapers until he heard that he could make 65 cents a round as a caddie. He had to fight to get a place and said that he would run seven miles to the course. Eventually he had one club, a left-handed mashie, and used to tear up the grass in the back yard until his mother would send him to the grocery store and he would hit shots along the road. When he changed to right-handed he said he had the most awful time, and that the effort used to nauseate him.

Hogan started professional golf when he was 18, and all the world knows of the years of struggle and hardship before he could win. His first major victory, the P.G.A. Championship, was not until 1946 when he was two years older than Nicklaus is now. Then, on the threshold of absolute supremacy, came the accident which nearly destroyed him, leaving its mark forever afterwards and compelling him to husband his resources and not tire himself socialising. The ensuing remoteness helped to compound a figure of legend, as indeed he became to a greater extent than any other golfer of his time. You could feel it whenever he appeared.

If Hogan walks into a room you are aware of a presence, although nothing of his manner or outward appearance attracts attention. Always he dresses impeccably, inconspicuously, in modest shades. Vivid colours and cheap gimmicks are not for Hogan; there is nothing about him of the extrovert effusiveness so common in the American male; always in public his manner is quiet and contained. More often than not in those later years he would be addressed as

Throughout his career Hogan commanded respect from spectators and fellow professionals alike.

Mr. Hogan; others were Arnie, Billy or Sam on the briefest acquaintance, but Hogan was Mr. and the title is more meaningful in America than in Britain. Similarly, on the course Hogan never sought acclaim for its own sake, or in any way played to the gallery. An army of screaming fans, like those on which Palmer thrives, meant nothing to him. He allowed his masterful golf to speak for itself and it usually did. The applause that greeted him as he approached every green had a note of respect reserved for no one else; the people, reverent rather than ecstatic, would clap rather than cheer.

There is no doubt that Hogan came closer than anyone to eliminating the human element from golf. Such was his control of the ball, and completeness of technique, and so true in outline and rhythm was his swing that he seemed immune to the pressures that destroy other golfers. When he was ahead in his great years his command of an event seemed unbreakable; rarely if ever was there any stumbling on the way to victory, such as that which has troubled Nicklaus on occasion and Bob Jones long ago. One of the few regrets that Jones had about his competitive golf was that he sometimes surrendered a commanding position and won far less easily than he should have done. Not so Hogan: as Jones himself said, "Ben was always so good at finishing the job."

Probably the greatest instance of this was in 1951 when Oakland Hills had been made savagely penal for the United States Open. Clayton Heafner with a 69 was the only other player to break 70 in the whole Championship. Hogan's scores read 76–73–71–67. The final round conceivably is the greatest he ever played, although when I asked him to confirm this years later he said: "It is very difficult to get your mind back on to one particular round, analyse it again and say whether it was better than any other one." This was revealing of the man in that he would estimate greatness by the quality of the shots rather than the winning of a championship. He went on to mention a round he had recently played, some of which I saw. Laurel Valley that day of the P.G.A. Championship was very long and heavy, but he missed no fairways and only one green by three yards, and was round in 70 having taken three putts five times. He thought he had played as well as ever he could; he was then 53.

No modern golfer has ever finished the job more emphatically than Hogan did in 1953. He won the Masters by five strokes with a total of 274 that only Nicklaus has beaten; the United States Open by six and the British by four. His golf at Carnoustie was so masterful that had his putting been fractionally better than moderate the Championship would have been no contest at all. His scores were 73–71–70–68, another ruthless downward progression, and one felt that had a fifth round been necessary it would have been 66. This was the peak of his supremacy.

Hogan won no more championships, but 10 years later the professionals were still saying that from tee to green he could hit the ball better than any man alive. But even Hogan, tough of spirit as he was, did not have an inexhaustible supply of nerve and gradually putting became an agony and a frustration to him and the worshipping watchers. Leaving the practice ground one morning at Augusta on his way to the putting green he said, "Now for the bloodbank," and he meant it.

In the third round of his last appearance in the Masters in 1967 Hogan, rising 55, played the back nine in 30, and the only putts holed of any length were from six, 15 and 25 feet. For thousands a lifetime's memory had been

Ben Hogan – the Greatest Ever?

"Would you like to share a car with Mr. Snead?" "Not particularly," said Hogan.

made, but the next day brought tiredness and reaction.

Hogan was the ultimate perfectionist, the more remarkable because he emerged from an age when intensive practice was not the fashion. Once, after a 64 in a tournament he practised for two hours and everyone thought "I was nuts." He practised with a ferocity of intent that can never have been surpassed, as if refusing to believe that it was not possible to create a flawless swing. There can never have been a more acute golfing intelligence than Hogan's, and for a great part of his lifetime he concentrated it upon the search for perfection.

I have the impression of him that hitting pure golf shots was the fulfilment of his whole being, as much an expression of his soul as a painting to an artist, a piece of music to a composer, and he was never satisfied. He saw no reason why every hole should not produce a birdie, and I could imagine his feelings when he dreamt one night that he had 17 holes in one, and one in two. Telling this he turned to me almost angrily and said, "When I woke up I was so goddam mad."

The pursuit of perfection was not confined to the golf course. When he began to manufacture clubs in 1954 he was so displeased with the output that he insisted on having it all destroyed. Nothing but the finest would appear under his name. The gesture cost the company a great deal of money, but Hogan's pride was satisfied.

The swing he created was not beautiful except in the sense that there is beauty in the smooth working of any machine. The backswing was compact and flatter than the classical concept, but the extension of the arc through the ball was quite remarkable with the right arm remaining straight through to the finish of the swing. The tempo was fastish; it was remote from the lazy effortless grace of Jones or Snead, but there was about it a wonderful sense of precision, like an instrument of flawlessly tempered steel.

For many years his accuracy was phenomenal. He could shape the shots as he willed, and even late in his career he could place drives as precisely as others would medium irons. To watch him fade or draw the ball ever so slightly, usually away from a hazard, was an unforgettable sight. The flight of his long irons had a searing quality, the ball so truly struck that it seemed motionless as if drawn down a plumb-line. If accurate striking be the measure of greatness then Hogan must be classed as the finest of all golfers. Gene Sarazen, who has played with every great player of the half-century since Vardon has often said that no one ever covered the flag like Hogan.

In 14 consecutive United States Opens up to 1960, and the same number of Masters to 1956 he was never outside the first 10, and was in the first four 18 times.

Of all the impressions of Hogan that memory cherishes those of him against the matchless background of Augusta are perhaps the strongest; many of the tees are cool places of green gold shadows, cloistered in the trees. Hogan, swarthy, silent and inscrutable, appears, tees his ball and takes his stance with that impression of massive authority created only by the great ones; the powerful hands, mahogany dark, mould themselves on the club, the swing coils and uncoils, swift and true as a lash of steel; the ball arrows away and Hogan with his stiff rather limping walk moves out of the shade. A moment later he stands in the sunfilled loneliness of the fairway. At such moments there was a rare quality of stillness about him and one could sense the absolute concentration of the cold, shrewd mind as he surveyed the shot.

"*I never get to use my putter.
I keep chipping them in.*"

8
Age is No Barrier to Golf Enjoyment

You've met him of course. The chap at the bar who tells you, with the air of pessimism, that you should realise the physical limitations that arrive with age and give the game up.

But you don't want to, do you? Quite right. Resist with every fibre in your body.

No need to go mad and overdo the physical bit by playing or practising more than is expected of anyone over the fifty mark, but neither do you have to let things stagnate.

Pay a little attention to keeping yourself in trim by using a series of simple exercises. Nothing strenuous, nothing likely to upset or tax the heart, but a few gentle exercises meant to strengthen just those muscles necessary to keep one hitting the ball with some degree of authority.

Let's break things down and take the hand and arm muscles first. The best way to reach these is to swing as you do in golf but with something heavier than your own clubs.

Much depends on what you have in the garden shed, but the rake is ideal. The hands and arms will do all the work of starting and stopping the rake as it moves through the path of a golf swing.

Its length, with the weight so far removed from the hands, will tire those muscles quickly. You need not repeat the exercise for too long. Maybe two or three minutes at a time, and the best time is just before going to bed.

Special heavy clubs have been made available for exercises of this nature, but, because of its stiffness and length, the rake is by far the better implement for the purpose. There is no "give" at all and to move it you must *move* the hands and arms, the whole object of the exercise. Swing the rake slowly at first and as you find your hands getting stronger you should swing faster.

Now we'll have a look at the legs. If you walk outdoors a lot, little attention will be needed, but for those who sit at a desk, or drive a car all day and get out on to a course only at week-ends, some toning exercises become essential.

Lie on the floor on your back. Draw the knees up to the abdomen, go on, a little further back than that, now extend your legs full length. Keep them there for a second. Point the toes without allowing the heels to touch the floor. You already feel better.

Do this a dozen times and you will be giving those leg muscles a good lengthening and stretching. It will do them good. Again do not overdo things. Start perhaps with ten, get to a dozen then work up slowly. Be reasonable at all times. If you can eventually get up to 20, be satisfied with that, and repeat the same number tomorrow.

A good aspect of the adoption of a programme of simple exercises is the general improvement that can be obtained in the control of nerves, so important on or around the green where any nervousness can be disheartening.

Having dealt with arms, hands and legs, we come to the trunk and spine where perhaps we meet with greater problems. The smooth hip action seems to disappear with age and so one finds it more difficult to stay over the ball through the swing.

Maybe one should have a word or two with the doctor as to the exercises to be adopted, but if you can find a strong bar some seven or eight feet off the floor you have the answer. Grasp the bar with the hands and lift yourself slowly off the floor to bring your chin level with the bar. This enables the weight of the legs to stretch the spine and vertebrae for a few moments . . . and it helps.

Golf itself has an odd way of compensating in skill and experience for any lack of yardage which every year brings in its wake.

You are not going to hit the ball as far as you did when young, but you can replace length with greater accuracy, and this in many cases is a telling factor.

Loss of length is the enemy of all golfers past the half-century mark, but you can counteract it by keeping fit, improving accuracy and spending a little more time studying the short game.

Take heart from the experience of the 80-year-old player, who daily, weather permitting, played his golf at Waterhall in Sussex. As the years progressed so the holes played diminished in number, but at 80 he was still managing 13 holes a day on a hilly course.

The first hole, some 180 yards, usually into a nasty cross-wind, he always tackled with a very, very old wood . . . and came the day when he did that hole in one . . . the first time in his life he had achieved such a feat. And at 80!

Golf is a game that can be played – and enjoyed – at any age.

FRANK BEARD *is one of golf's leading money-winners without ever becoming a feted super-star. Quiet man of the tour he has a quick mind and a sharp sense of humour.*

PETER OOSTERHUIS, *leader of Britain's Order of Merit in 1971 and one of this country's brightest prospects for future international stardom.*

BRIAN BARNES, *the big-hitting Briton who*
finished fifth in the 1972 Open at Muirfield.

BILLY CASPER *(right) who has failed*
consistently to make any real impression on British
golf despite a great record in America.

MAURICE BEMBRIDGE *(left) Britain's most travelled young professional. Winner last year of the Dunlop Masters title.*

ROBERTO DE VICENZO, *a tremendous favourite with golf spectators throughout the world. Winner of the British Open in 1967 at Hoylake.*

PETER TOWNSEND, *one of Britain's finest amateur golfers, has a superb professional record in Britain and Europe, yet has failed to make his mark in America.*

9 How to Beat the Club Champion

So you want to beat the club champion? That is natural enough. We all do.

Of course, being a low-handicap player he has a pretty big psychological advantage over a lesser golfer such as yourself, but there are chinks in the armour.

You are approaching the first tee. Remember you are *not* beaten at that stage. Think that way and you can turn right round and go back to the changing room without putting a club in your hand.

Certainly he is going to hit his shots better than you, but among them will be a few a little below his usual standard. If you strive to get the maximum out of your own shots, you are still very much in the picture.

He's not infallible you know, and scratch-men don't play to their handicaps every time. Think on that one. And he's got much less margin for error than you!

Don't be nervous. Forget his superiority in shot power, and never feel apologetic about any difference in ability. He is not expecting you to play as well as him, otherwise he'd be asking you for shots.

Another thing. Don't get to the course too early and hang around doing nothing. Get there in time to change without haste. Keep calm, get to the tee a minute or so before time after a few loosening-up practice swings. Look confident and you'll feel confident.

See that your equipment is in good shape, too. Shabby dress, ill-kept clubs covered in mud, and the champ will give you a look that will freeze you into a nervous state, likely to last for the first five holes – by which time it's too late anyway.

Try to meet him on equal sartorial and equipment terms. It is so much more satisfying.

Remember not to rush things. Take everything calmly and slowly. Take your time, and don't panic. Obey any rules in existence regarding the honour. Don't let him have the honour just because he's the better player. Sort that out right away, even if you have to toss for it.

Put down a new ball, straight from its wrapping. It's a big day for you and you need every assistance you can get.

Note where your opponent's ball is in relation to yours. He may have hit it further, but that does not mean he has an easier second shot than yours. Think about this, and remember you have a stroke to play with. Consider every shot on its merits.

We all have some special skill or other in our game. It might be putting, chipping or driving accurately, but whatever it is try to make the maximum use of your speciality. Above all, play your own game within your own limitations. Just remember that if you play to your handicap, the champion must play below his to beat you.

It is on or around the greens where you can really be on equal terms. Do not assume the champion is going to hole every short putt and start conceding two or three-footers. He has to hole them all – so keep him under pressure.

Keep your temper. That's really important. Get rattled and you are beaten. If your opponent shows signs of tantrums, ignore him, and concentrate even more on your own game. It's your golden opportunity.

If you have a lead, don't become complacent or over-confident. Never ease back when facing a better player. If two up, try hard to make it three up.

It doesn't pay to grumble if things go wrong. It wastes energy, and gives a point to the other side. Pull yourself out of it and keep plugging away. Do your damndest to win, and when you are enjoying a victory drink – be modest about it.

Congratulations . . . Champ!

10 Instant Improvement

through Self-Analysis

John Jacobs

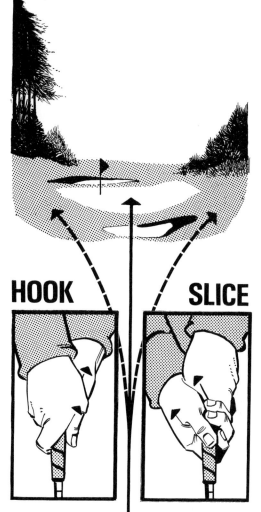

Without setting foot on the golf course or practice ground every golfer knows the basic pattern of his normal shots – whether the ball moves from left to right or from right to left in the air. In the majority of cases it will be a left-to-right slice with which he has to contend.

Read the following pages carefully and you will be able to eliminate the most destructive shots in your golf game the next time you play. The knowledge of the shape of your standard golf shot, together with the corrective information in this self-analysis article, can make you a better golfer overnight.

There is only one reason why a golf ball will bend in the air – because it has been hit with an open or closed club-face. An open club-face will cause the ball to move from left to right – in golfing terms a slice – and a closed club-face will cause a bend from right to left – a hook.

The majority of golfers seem determined to over-complicate the golf swing – so much so that they will tend to doubt the simplicity of my last statement. Yet it is a golfing fact.

If the club-face is square to the line of the swing the ball will fly straight through the air. It will not always fly straight at the target – but that is a different matter. Only if the club-face is pointing right or left of the line of swing will the ball turn in the air.

This means that the first priority in any practice plan is to move the position of the hands on the grip of the club so that it delivers

HOOK

SLICE

If you hook the ball move the hands to the left on the grip until ball flies straight right of target.

If you slice the ball, move hands to the right on the grip until ball flies straight left of target.

SLICE

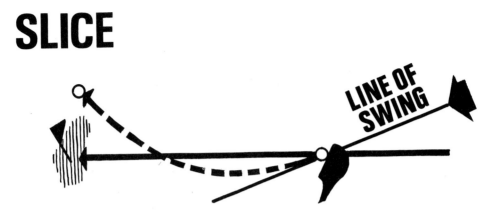

the club-face square to the line of swing at impact with the ball. If you slice, move your hands to the right as you look down at the grip of the club. Experiment with this stronger grip until the flight of the ball is straight – no matter what direction the ball takes. Almost certainly it will fly straight left of the target at which you are aiming. This is quite natural, for the automatic reaction to hitting the ball with an open club-face and therefore curving the ball to the right, is to aim further and further left in order to keep the ball on the fairway. This leads to a swing path which comes from outside to inside the target line. Your swing is aiming left of the target, but because the club-face is open the ball is finishing to the right of the target. This out-to-in swing path is the opposite of what is required in a good golf swing.

By hitting the ball straight through the air, you now have the club-face aimed in the same direction as the swing path. But if the swing path is to the left of the target, that is exactly where the ball will finish. Yet once you start consistently hitting the ball left of where you are aiming, it is a perfectly natural

PULL

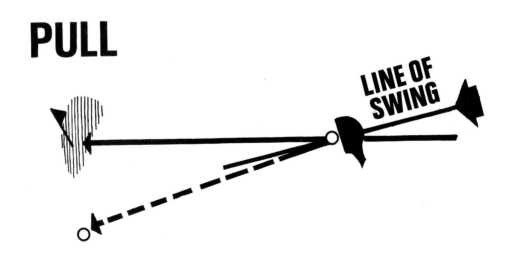

HOOK

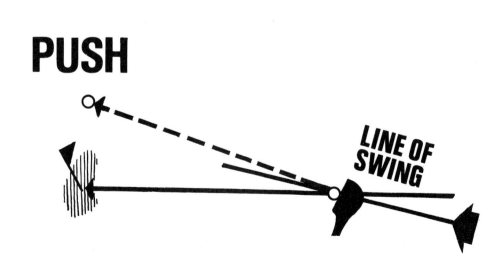

LINE OF SWING

reaction to swivel the whole address position round until the body and swing path are aimed at the target. This alone will overcome the out-to-in swing path and lead to a natural adjustment to the correct swing path which is from slightly inside the line from ball to target as it approaches the ball, straight through along the target line for a short spell through impact, and then inside the line again once the ball has been hit.

For those golfers who hook the ball, moving it from right to left in the air, the hands should be moved to the left on the grip until the ball flies straight. This time it will almost certainly fly to the right of the target. This indicates that at impact the club-face is square to the line of the swing, but that the swing path is aimed to the right of the target to allow for the accustomed right-to-left movement of the ball.

A hooker's swing is almost always too much from inside the line through the ball to the target, but once you start to hit the ball to the right of the target, the automatic reaction is to aim more to the left – and once again a natural cure is in progress.

PUSH

LINE OF SWING

STRAIGHT SHOTS

For a straight shot the clubface must be square to the line of the swing and square to the target line at impact. The best way to achieve this is with the feet and shoulders square to the target line at address and with the Vs formed between the thumb and forefinger of each hand pointing between the chin and the right shoulder at address. The path of the swing is from inside to straight through and inside again on the follow through. The ball must be positioned so that the clubhead makes contact while it is on the straight part of the swing arc.

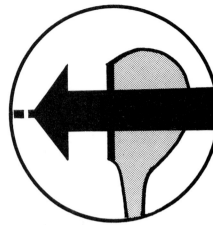

FADE

When deliberately trying to fade the ball, the clubface must be open to the line of the swing path at impact. The swing path should be out-to-in for a fade and the ball will therefore start to the left and fade back to the target. By positioning the ball further forward in the stance than normal the club will make contact with the ball when it is swinging from out-to-in. By placing the ball further forward the shoulders will be in an open position at address and this will also tend to weaken the grip — turning both hands to the left on the club shaft and encouraging an open clubface at impact.

DRAW

In an attempt to draw the ball it should be positioned further back in the stance than normal, allowing contact to be made on an in-to-out path. With the clubface closed this sets the ball off to the right and draws it back to the target. By positioning the ball further back in the stance the shoulders become closed and the grip strengthens, with both hands moving to the right on the club shaft. This promotes a closed clubface at impact.

11 How Golf Balls are made

The modern golf ball, being a highly developed object, deserves all the attention it receives, and it is no surprise to find it has undergone more changes than any other item of the game's implements.

Take the centre filling. Over the years substances used have included water, various viscous pastes, blood, steel, pills, rubber, glass fibre, silicone, iodine, mercury, dry ice, tapioca, gelatine and arsenic.

Even today more people throughout the world are engaged on its manufacture than any other department of the game's equipment, and experiments are continuous.

And it is all for us.

Whatever is felt about golfing tradition or the old-style manners and playing methods, everyone is seeking to buy skill. The ball gives the better chance of the better score. The further and straighter it flies, the more likely, we believe, we are to play well.

At the present time, there is interest in at least three aspects of the golf ball. Its quality, its ultimate potential in terms of performance, and its price, but we will deal with these points further on.

Meanwhile a few facts and figures.

It is the winding of the rubber thread, put on under tension, that builds up and stores the energy. It has been said that there is enough energy in the winding to lift an 11-stone man two feet off the ground, and pressure at the centre of the completed ball is about 2,500 pounds per square inch.

Moment of impact. Compression by the club-head gives the ball its energy to fly. The speed of the club-head is about 100 m.p.h. The picture was taken at half a millionth of a second. (Pictures by permission of Dunlop.)

Every time you hit that ball, the thread is stretched and so some energy is lost.

Have you ever attempted to count those dimples? They are vitally important and generally number about 330 with a depth of 0·0135 of an inch and any alteration in the depth, even by 0·001 of an inch will drastically affect flight and distance.

If 0·002 of an inch shallower than the optimum, a ball that flies 240 yards on a normal drive would fly 20–30 yards shorter, and the shallower the dimples the more erratic the flight.

When well struck with a driver a golf ball spins counter-clockwise at 30 revolutions a second. A nine iron spins it at 160 revolutions a second and it is this backspin which gives the ball its lift.

In America, a key word in golf-ball selling is "compression" – with golfers at all stages ever anxious to find the compression most suited to their swing. Compression relates to the hardness of the ball. A high compression denotes a hard ball which requires a powerful blow to obtain maximum performance. A low compression means a softer ball from which maximum performance can be gained with a lesser impact force.

British manufacturers fight shy of compression, but balls are tested throughout manufacture to ensure they conform to the manufacturer's own optimum compression. Those not complying because they are too soft become second-grade balls, and strangely enough it is possible that such balls are more suited to many golfers' abilities than the higher compression top-grade balls.

Generally speaking the faster the club-head is applied, the higher compression ball can be used to maximum effect . . . and vice versa.

"Feel" plays an important part, and also the matter of control. A hard golf ball feels just that and so comes fast off the club-face. A soft golf ball is flattened more by the club-face to which it adheres longer, giving a satisfying "feel" and possibly more control.

Size?

For many years the question of diameter change has been the main topic of conversation in clubhouse get-togethers. Should it remain at 1·62 or increase to 1·68? Or will we all be forced to use the compromise 1·66 that is threatened?

When the subject was first raised, general reaction among British golfers was apathetic, despite the R. and A.'s plea to give the big ball an extensive trial. There was also, understandably, a certain amount of trade reaction against it.

Since then we have seen a slight swing to-wards its use, even at club level. Manu-facturers are better equipped to deal with both sizes, and so satisfy home and export demand, but there is still a big question mark as to its value as an aid to improve playing standards.

Dr. Alistair Cochran, chairman of the scientific panel appointed by the Golf Society to probe the golf swing, and writing in the Society's *Bulletin* in 1964 had this to say of the American-sized golf ball: ". . . While as claimed the big ball flies higher the difference is a matter of only three feet on a drive. When sliced or hooked it does deviate more than the small ball, but only by about six per cent."

Commenting on performance on greens, Dr. Cochran said: "No difference could be detected either by observing the behaviour of the ball or by exhaustive tests in which

Measuring out the clay and water paste used in the centres.

Core winding strips of extremely thin rubber are wound on to the centres. Most of the ball's energy is stored in the winding, 30 yards unstretched, extended by 900 per cent when finished.

more than 4,000 putts were struck by golfers of all abilities."

He ended with this note: "By all means let us have trials, and if golfers on the whole prefer the larger ball, let us adopt it permanently. But do not let us imagine by doing so we are ensuring playing superiority or even parity in world golf."

Eight years later there are many still who will agree with all these points, and that is following many thousands of rounds of golf played in varying weather conditions.

So arguments are bound to continue.

Ultimate potential? We now have a far-flying ball well suited to the power techniques of the top echelon of players, and all research, which is constant and exhaustive, is designed to improve that ball in every way. Especially the distance it will fly.

And there can be little doubt "long" balls

After the covers, in the form of two half-cups, are added to the core, the final moulding, where the balls acquire their dimples, takes place. The pattern and depth of the dimples affect the behaviour in flight. A Dunlop "65" has 332.

Before final inspection, balls are tested automatically for size, weight and compression.

Balls receive two coats of paint from spray-guns which swing through an arc as the balls perch on rotating prongs. Polyurethane paint sticks well, looks good and resists cracking.

sell, and sell fast, providing one can be sure of consistency of performance, lasting qualities and even appearance. Fortunately the golf trade in Britain, being very much part of the game with the game's interest at heart, is fully alert to all such factors.

The "souped-up" golf ball may reach headlines elsewhere, but it could well prove a disappointment on the majority of British courses, established as they were in the days of the gutty.

As with everything else the price of golf balls seem to rise, but the increase in the cost relative to other goods has been small. Thanks for this must lie with the continually increasing demand, research and development.

While material and production costs increase rather than diminish they can be offset by increased output, while modern competition among manufacturers also has a bearing.

And even if a ball lasts only one round, rate of expenditure is perhaps 30p for three hours' recreation. That's not too bad, is it?

The end of the line. Hot-foil stamping before the application of clear lacquer, then packing and away.

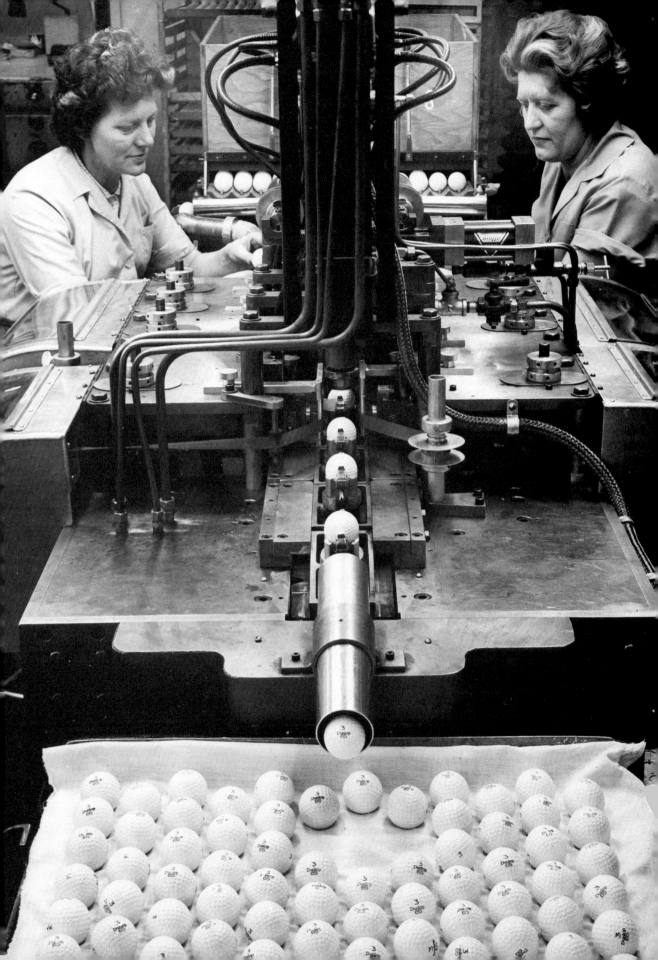

12 Trevino's Swing Sequence

LEE TREVINO positions the ball well forward in his
stance, with feet, hips and shoulders in an open position.
His open stance is more pronounced with the short irons

as shown here, but applies to the long irons and woods
as well. From this set-up position the club is taken away
slightly outside the direct ball-to-target line.

At the top of the backswing with the short and medium irons Trevino sets the club-face open, which enables him to draw these shots slightly without fear of a

punishing hook. With the longer clubs he has the club-
face more closed at the top which, with his open set-up,
allows him to fade the ball while guarding against a slice

Although he tends to take the club away slightly outside the line, Trevino drops it back very quickly at the start of the downswing, coming at the ball from the inside with

**the left side moving well out of the way to allow room
for the long extension of right arm and shoulder through
impact. He is very repetitive and solid through the ball**

13 The State of the

*Can golf's traditions survive
the seventies?*

Herbert Warren Wind

These are unpredictable times, and no one knows what lies ahead for golf. It may continue to grow and become an even more lustrous part of the national and global scene. Or, for no apparent reason, it may suddenly lose its privileged place in the scheme of things, like baseball, piano lessons, the polo coat, the well-made Broadway play, the Packard, penmanship, railroad travel, dance music, the bakery wagon and countless other faded glories that in earlier eras loomed as unshakeable as the English pound and the American Legion. Accordingly, I think it would be an excellent idea if we paused for a moment and reflected on the golden age of golf we have lived through in the quarter of a century since sports were revived in earnest at the close of World War II. Here are just a few of the things that happened in the 25 years between 1946 and 1971:

1. Not that figures tell everything, but the number of golfers increased as never before – in the United States from 3 million to 10 million, in the world from 8 million to 20 million. Similarly, the number of courses in the U.S. rose from under 5,000 to over 10,000, and in the world from under 8,000 to over 15,000. (A hundred years ago, by the way, there were fewer than 50 golf clubs in the

American Game

[See panel overleaf]

whole world. A mere handful lay beyond the borders of Scotland, and there was not a single one on this side of the Atlantic.)

2. The total prize-money on the American tournament circuit in 1947 came to $352,500. Today it has climbed to over $7,250,000. In 1947 Jimmy Demaret was the leading money winner on the tour with a haul of $27,936.83. In 1971 a dozen golfers earned over $100,000 on the American tour – *and no fewer than 79 earned over $27,936.83.*

3. Since the war, such significant new international competitions as the World Cup (for two-man professional teams), the Eisenhower Trophy (for four-man amateur teams) and the Espirito Santo Trophy (for three-woman amateur teams) have solidly established themselves. They have not been completely dominated by the traditional golf powers either. Argentina (1953), Australia (1954, 1959 and 1970), Japan (1957), Ireland (1958), South Africa (1965) and Canada (1968) all have won the World Cup (originally the Canada Cup). France has won the women's team championship.

4. Where the modern champions are concerned, one can go on and on dealing in warranted superlatives. In this period Ben Hogan reached the climax of his career. While Harry Vardon and Bob Jones should

"A hundred years ago there were fewer than 50 golf clubs in the world – a mere handful lay beyond the borders of Scotland.
Today there are in excess of 15,000 courses and 20 million golfers."

Early pros like Harry Vardon (1) and Old Tom Morris (2) played for only a few hundred dollars. Later, amateurs Walter Travis (3), Francis Ouimet (4) and Bob Jones (5) played simply for the love of competition. Walter Hagen (6) was reputedly the first to earn $1 million from golf. His successors, such as Gene Sarazen (7), Byron Nelson (8), Ben Hogan (9) and Sam Snead (10), have prospered from the game, but never to the extent now enjoyed by multi-millionaires Arnold Palmer (11) and Jack Nicklaus (12). Fortunately, despite their business

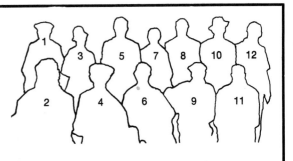

involvements, both Palmer and Nicklaus retain a sincere love and respect for the game's traditions.

be rated Hogan's equals – after all, they accomplished as much in their times as he did in his – Hogan, with the assistance of modern equipment stands by himself as the finest striker of the ball and the most accurate shotmaker the game has ever known.

This period also produced Arnold Palmer, perhaps the most exciting figure to appear on the American sports scene. Under a new U.S.G.A. rule, anyone using the word *"charisma"* in writing about Palmer is henceforth subject to a two-stroke penalty, so we will content ourselves with saying that Palmer's appeal has been so extraordinary that he has made contact with everyone – young and old, male and female, golfer and non-golfer, American and foreigner, poet and labourer. In doing so, he widened the game's appeal and brought to it its largest audience ever.

In addition, there is Jack Nicklaus, an unprecedented combination of sophisticated power and spectacular technique. Jack has had more crests and valleys in his career than most tournament golfers, but when he has been at the top of his game he has several times unleashed a sustained brilliance that no other player in the long history of golf has approached. This, of course, is what Bob Jones had in mind when he remarked in 1965, after Nicklaus had broken practically all the records for the Masters Tournament, "Jack Nicklaus is playing an entirely different game – a game I'm not even familiar with."

There is no question that Peter Thomson, who won five British Opens between 1954 and 1965, is the greatest Australian golfer of all time. There is little question that Gary Player, who won five major championships between 1959 and 1968, is the greatest South African golfer of all time – a notch superior to the remarkable Bobby Locke.

One could go on and on, but let us leave it at this, for the point must be amply clear: in the last quarter of a century, golf has prospered mightily in just about every way. For some observers, it reached an untoppable peak when Alan Shepard assembled his trusty six-iron on the surface of the moon, though others were even more impressed when King Hassan II of Morocco summoned his favourite playing pro, Billy Casper, for a practice session less than two weeks after he had survived a palace uprising in the summer of 1971. And then, to be sure, there is that separate school of thought which believes that the game has exhibited its fibre most conspicuously in the way it has survived the devotion of Spiro Agnew.

I mention all this because a main purpose of this article is to point out that, despite its voluminous prosperity and overall health, there are quite a few directions in which golf is moving these days that are cause for concern. To say it another way, a good many of the finest things about golf are in the process of being forgotten. Change, of course is inevitable. Frequently it is beneficial, though this is not always the case. In any event, the people who are involved in golf should at least be more aware than most of them are of new trends and forces that have come into the game. What I hope to do here is discuss the changing scene in some detail and try to put the good things and the bad things about it in a reasonable perspective. We will deal with the pro tour, television, the demise of match-play, the threats to the country club, slow play, the golf car and the caddie, teaching, the decline in etiquette, the rules, course architecture and the present penchant for over-indulging college golfers.

To begin with, I should confess that, for me, the atmosphere in and around tournament golf has lost a good deal of its old sporting flavour. As I see it, this has come about to a large extent because there is too much money in professional golf nowadays. Curiously, it is not the *amount* of the prize-money that bothers me – that is not out of line with purses and salaries in other sports or, for that matter, with what the leaders in business and other professions are currently making. At the same time, it is probably the huge increases in prize-money over the past decade – in 1960, remember, a $50,000 tournament was a whopper – that account for the almost institutionalised decorum with which most circuit pros now go about their appointed rounds. To mix a metaphor, they seem to be walking on egg-shells, only too well aware of what a good thing professional golf is and eternally vigilant lest they do anything that might kill the goose that lays the golden eggs. "Tournament golf has become so cut and dried that I don't enjoy watching it on television any more," a friend of mine, a non-golfer, was explaining recently. "Practically every guy has the same set of gestures. They all walk on to the green the same way. They all line up their putts the same way. If they hole the putt, they all turn on the same kind of a smile and tip their hat the same way. When they're interviewed they all say the same thing: they were 'fortunate to play so well this week against this fine group of gentlemen.' It's all so calculated and unspontaneous that it's positively eerie." I think my friend goes too far, but there is more than a germ of truth in what he says.

For myself, one aspect of the financial picture that worries me is that tournament prize-money is comparatively small pickings compared to the sums a champion can make from television commercials and other product endorsements. In order to break through the barrier that separates the merely success- ful touring pro from a sports hero like Palmer and thus qualify for the really big money, a golfer must not only demonstrate that he has the ability to win a major championship (the U.S. Open, the British Open, the Masters or the P.G.A.) but also show that he has the stuff to get across to the public as a Personality with a capital P – someone who you and I want to identify with, consciously or subconsciously; someone who has such a strong appeal for us that if, say, he drives a white Essex, we'll want to drive a white Essex.

As a result, what we have today in the tournament world is a situation where a number of the players just below the first five appear to be much more interested in improving their images than in improving their golf. To exaggerate a bit for effect, here, moving up the fairway, comes Phil Familyman followed by as many of his nine children as the tournament officials will allow inside the ropes. Phil is obviously devoted to them. In the next twosome, bestowing that nonstop smile on the spectators, we have Glenn Golden who is trying desperately to get himself across as the personification of youth, blondness and a sunny disposition. Compared to Glenn, the Man from Glad is grubby and negative. Coming into view now with that choppy, rugged stride is Hardy Competitor, a fellow who wants the fans to know that he never stops fighting and who has worked up a large repertoire of gestures and cries that transmit this admirable quality. For instance, when Hardy saw how warmly the spectators responded when Gary Player punched the air with his fist after holing a good-sized putt, he devised that marvellous variation whereby he punches the air with a left jab, a right uppercut and a left hook, in that order. And so on and on. (Who said there weren't individuals on the tour!) Among the new acts, the most successful by far is Lee Trevino's,

and while granting Trevino's natural charm and ebullience, I am inclined to think that it owes its success to the fact that he is such an astonishing golfer. It brings one back to Walter Hagen. If he had not been such a great shotmaker, he would not have been such a great showman.

The more that golf becomes a branch of the entertainment world and a means to an end rather than an end in itself, the more it is bound to surrender that rare and special flavour that the world of sports possesses when it is at its best. Some people love it, of course, when a Dave Hill is in an eloquently rude mood, or a Cliff Richey tears up the taped line of a tennis court to dramatise his wrath over a linesman's call, or a Muhammad Ali throws a tantrum at a weigh-in. For them, this is Colour. The true sports fan, I suggest, finds these moments uncomfortable and irrelevant. They are not what drew him to the event. Colour for him is function. It is there inevitably when skilful athletes perform their dazzling deeds. For him, consequently, golfers are most glamorous when they are totally absorbed in playing golf.

Quite often these days when I am watching a fine young golfer who is wooing his gallery all too deliberately, I find myself thinking of Ben Hogan; for if ever a man epitomised the Old School, it is Hogan. There were stretches in his career, in fact, when his demeanour on the course was undoubtedly too severe. With his enormous pride and his passion for perfection, Ben couldn't stand to play poor golf, and whenever he struck a really bad patch, he would pack up and leave the tour, head for the practice tee and slave away monastically until he had corrected the cause of his trouble and was back on his stick again. The idea of continuing to play tournaments at these times because he might pick up a little prize-money or gain some other commercial benefit – this was anathema to him. No different from anyone else, Hogan wanted to make money through his golf, but his standards were exceedingly high. With Hogan, golf came first, and he gave it everything he had. You felt this whenever you saw him in action, and this is what made watching him such an incisive and indelible experience.

It is impossible to overstate the power of television or overemphasise its influence on our lives. There are times when television seems more real than life itself – as if it were the substance and life were the shadow. Each year the feeling grows among all of us that if something isn't shown on television, then it just didn't happen.

Television has affected all sports to a considerable degree, but none quite as much as golf. To begin on a light note, it has, we noted earlier, dictated a whole new style of deportment for tournament players. Over the first 14 holes of his round, a player who is either in the throes of a bad slump or simply having a bad day may make no effort to hide his irritation with himself and the world in general. After a poor shot, he may toss his club petulantly towards his caddie. After a good shot, he may take elaborate pains to ignore the applause of his gallery. However, once he reaches the tee on the 15th hole (or whatever is the first hole on which the TV cameras are positioned), bingo, off goes the Mr. Hyde grimace and on comes that winning Dr. Jekyll smile. His manners are impeccable. You sense that, deep down, this man has integrity. If he ran a prep school, you would send your son there, no questions asked.

Television's greatest disservice to golf, perhaps, is that it has helped to virtually eliminate match-play as a form of competi-

tion for the game's best players. At the present time the pros engage in match-play in this country only in the newly revised version of the U.S. Professional Match-play Championship and every four years when it is our turn to host the Ryder Cup. The amateurs have a few more opportunities for match-play, but it is significant that since 1965 the U.S. Amateur Championship has been conducted at stroke-play, although match-play is the original form of golf and the traditional method of determining a national amateur champion. As a general rule, match-play is more fascinating to watch than stroke-play, but because the shape it can take is so unpredictable, it just doesn't suit television. How can a network make plans to televise live the finishing holes of a 36-hole match – until 1965 the format of the Amateur called for just such a final – when there is a fair chance that one of the players may wrap it up, say, 9 and 8 or 8 and 6 when the show has barely gone on the air. You're locked out then; there is no other action on the course to turn to.

If we are generally denied the excitement of match-play, it is wrong to imply that it is all television's fault. Long before the medium was sufficiently advanced technically to consider doing golf, the pros, as individuals, were looking for a good excuse to do away with match-play as the format of the P.G.A. Championship. Over 18 holes even the best player in the world can lose to a man with a hot putter, and it is rough enough for a star's self-esteem to get beaten in a head-to-head encounter by his peers, let alone by some upstart bumpkin. When a friend calls over to a name pro and asks him how he came out, how galling it is for him to have to answer, "I lost 3 and 2." It is all so definite, so pejorative. How much nicer and unbruis-

"In 1947 Jimmy Demaret was the leading money-winner on the American tour with a haul of $27,936 from a total prize fund of $352,500. In 1971 a dozen golfers earned more than $100,000 – and no fewer than 79 earned more than Demaret's 1947 total of $27,936."

ing it is, after he shoots a similarly mediocre round in a stroke-play tournament, to be able to answer the same question, with an attractive shake of the head, "Three over, can you believe it? Hit the ball perfectly but couldn't buy a putt. Must have missed half a dozen under four feet." (I am convinced, by the way, that the reason tennis players are so taut and temperamental during a tournament – off the court as well as on – is that there is no such face-saving luxury as stroke-play competition in tennis. The threat of losing a match hangs continually over the head of the tennis player, and that makes for enormous pressure.)

Then, too, our national organisations, the P.G.A. and U.S.G.A., must shoulder a fair share of the blame for the passing of the match-play championships. Of course, they do need money to operate, and in this day when the television networks aren't particularly interested in contracting the rights to a match-play event, you can understand why these associations have veered toward stroke-play. The P.G.A. actually began veering that way many long years ago, for all too often its match-play championship proved a financial bust. If Sam Snead and the one or two other gate attractions were eliminated in the early rounds, the public stayed away in droves the rest of the week. As for the U.S.G.A., there is no knowing how much weight the negotiation of its first big TV contract carried in that organisation's decision to change the Amateur to stroke-play, but even allowing that this move may have been of considerable financial importance to the U.S.G.A., I am not sure it was the right move. It is ironic, I think, that, aside from the Open, the favourite U.S.G.A. events of most of the U.S.G.A. officials I know are the Walker Cup and the Girls' Junior Championship, both conducted at match-play.

One final point which, while it has nothing to do with match-play, is extremely relevant. At the same time that the Amateur was changed to stroke-play, the U.S.G.A. made a revolutionary alteration in the Open, dispensing with the traditional double round of 36 holes on the third and final day and adopting the format of a single round on four days. I would suppose that gaining another day's television audience and, with that, a more bountiful television contract had something to do with this move. For many of us, however, this was a mistake, because we feel that the Open was a better championship when it required 36 holes on the last day. There are any number of golfers who can get through 18 holes even on an Open course without their swings coming apart, but 36 is an entirely different proposition: if your swing has a basic flaw, it will disintegrate under the attrition of that ever increasing pressure. Only a truly sound golfer can stand up to it, which is the way it should be in the national championship. As a result, the old Opens developed a drama all their own. As someone or other said once – it was either Andra Kirkaldy or Chairman Mao – when the U.S.G.A. revamped the Open, it lost a championship and gained just another tournament.

It comes down to this, more or less. During the past decade, it has often looked as if the whole world was turning itself inside out just to accommodate television camera crews. The golf world certainly has, at moments. It is about time that it realised that its first responsibility is to further the best expression of golf.

There's no need to worry about television; it will adjust. For example, if the U.S.G.A. decided to return to the climactic double round in the Open, the network telecasting the event would undoubtedly accord the championship at least as much air time, and possibly more, than it is presently getting. This isn't meant to imply that it would be an equally simple matter to get the networks to cover match-play golf as stroke-play golf, but should the major associations reintroduce pure match-play at a significant level, it would be surprising if the networks didn't quickly learn how to cope with the new and special problems involved. After all, light portable equipment is where television is heading, and even with the present largely stationary equipment, the B.B.C. does a pretty fair job covering the annual eight--man-field Piccadilly World Match-play Championship.

The laws of civilisation are inexorable, apparently, and those of us who are still around in the year 2000 are bound to look back at the early 1970s as the Good Old Days. I certainly trust that at that time we will not be bewailing the fact that you cannot find a good golf course any more in our villages and cities, all of them having been forced to close down due to the steadily climbing tax bases and other unstemmable financial burdens. It could happen, though, and golf could be pushed far out into the country and revert to being a sort of cousin of canoeing – which, on second thoughts, wouldn't be too bad if we could all get out and play as regularly as we would like to.

Golf has become such an expensive game today that it seems inconceivable that it can grow much more expensive. I suppose it will, though, and in line with the theory that these are the Good Old Days, the folks in the year 2000 will eat their hearts out when they come upon old diaries and read about the bargains we are enjoying at the present time.

In recent years, whipsawed by continuing inflation and the most serious business recession in decades, we have all come to appreciate

with alarming clarity how much money it takes to run a club where golf is played, be it a country club or just a plain golf club.

We also have come to appreciate how much it costs to belong to one. The truth of the matter, however, is that the golf has always been a costly sport in the United States. The country club, lest we forget, is an American invention. In England and Scotland down through the years, the people who played golf usually lived in the country to begin with. They customarily entertained each other privately, and so all that they needed in the way of clubhouse facilities was (a) a peg to hang their coat on, (b) a bench to sit on while changing their shoes and (c) a bar to lean on while having a small whisky or a pink gin.

In the United States, on the other hand, at the time when golf was introduced here late in the 19th century, the well-heeled people who were oriented towards sport usually dwelt in our cities. Accordingly, they had to get out to the country first, and the way they generally did this was by horse and carriage, driving out in the morning and back in the late afternoon. Before beginning the return journey, they would stop for food and drink at some inn or road-house unless they were lucky enough to have a friend or relative they could drop in on and regale with their delightful company.

These were the reasons why The Country Club in Brookline, Mass. – the first real country club – was founded in 1882. The Country Club offered the men who joined it good facilities for horse-racing, archery, shooting, lawn tennis, ice-skating, curling and, from 1893 on, golf. It provided, in addition, comfortable surroundings in which the members and their families could refresh themselves – all this in the company of their friends and for a comparatively modest outlay. Small wonder that once the craze for golf set in the 1890s, country clubs sprang up on the periphery of every self-respecting city in the land. As the nation grew more and more prosperous, the American country club became increasingly luxurious. By the twenties, they were pocket spas.

The Depression brought an end to all this. The clubs that survived it had learned a bitter lesson, and after that, even when the tide of affluence was swirling full force in the post-World War II years, only a few resumed their old extravagant ways. They couldn't very well, not with their property taxes growing constantly higher and with the cost of labour shooting up well beyond anyone's anticipations. Today, however prudent they may have been, many of our private clubs are once again in serious financial trouble. I am not an economist, so I will not attempt to develop this picture in detail and will simply set down a few statements of fact I have run across which seem to pack the real pith of the matter.

Many clubs are being forced to pay much higher property taxes because they are now assessed on the basis of "best land use" and not on the old basis of "recreational use", this can mean an increase of 500 PER CENT. (A club in the Cincinnati area, for example, had its assessment whomped up from $58,000 to $304,000.)

In the last two years the operating costs of the average private club have gone up just about 20 per cent. The cost of labour has been chiefly responsible for this.

Under the Tax Reform Act of 1969, golf clubs can now be taxed on all non-membership income. In the last 15 years, golf-course maintenance has jumped 85 per cent. Where the average cost of maintenance per hole was $2,559 in 1954, by 1969 it was up to $4,577. Of this, $2,824 went for labour.

The prospect is not too bright. Feeling the economic pinch, the average member is spending less at the club bar and in the dining room. Furthermore, the younger generation, which used to love to hang out at the country club, now finds the whole institution ungroovy and sometimes even repellent.

How does this translate in terms of the average club member? If he lives in a section of the country that has not been affected fundamentally by the population explosion or the fanning out of industry, his golf probably costs him between $350 and $600 a year, everything included, which isn't bad. However, his counterpart who lives in the suburbs of a sizeable city is taking a sweet tootsy-fruitsying these days. His annual dues are now up in the neighbourhood of $1,000. His locker costs him about $75 a year. He is often required to pay an annual charge of about $75 for storing his clubs in the pro shop (whether or not he stores them there), and he is usually slapped with a minimum charge each month of about $15 for food and drink (even in those months when the course is covered with three inches of snow and is slightly unplayable).

Without putting these extra bites on the members, some clubs would not have sufficient funds to meet their expenses, but on top of this, as nearly all of us know, clubs still find themselves in the red every so often and must impose assessments which run into the hundreds of dollars. . . . Yes, something is lost in the translation – close to $2,000 a year per golfer when you throw in the cost of golf balls, some new clubs periodically (at $40 for a top-quality wood and $30 for a top-quality iron), caddies at $6 or $7 per round, the rental of golf cars, buckets of practice balls, green fees for guests, an occasional lesson and tips.

The point of this lengthy recitation is this: *for many American golfers, it now costs too much to play golf*. What are the solutions? They will vary with each individual club, as they did in the Depression years. For some, the best policy will be to increase the size and scope of their operations so that each member and his family spend the maximum number of hours and dollars at the club; for others, the soundest procedure will be to get rid of all the overheads and become golf clubs, pure and simple. Since most of our clubs would probably fall into this second category, it might be wise for them to study the methods of operating that have enabled golf clubs in Great Britain and Ireland to keep the cost of golf well within the reach of the average citizen.

To start with, the clubs in the British Isles have kept down the cost of services, which is so critical, by settling for a very unplush mode of life in and around the clubhouse. If the club has a dining room, it will generally serve only lunch and tea, and there will be nothing fancy about the food, the service or the décor. The bar, however, will be open in the evening, because people like to drink at that time of day and also because the bar is a money-making proposition.

If British and Irish golf clubs are such austere places by our standards, I would suppose that it is chiefly because even now most of them are still male sanctuaries and not family hangouts. It is next to impossible to picture several tables of women chattily playing mah-jong in the big room of the R. and A., or a gang of kids clustered around a swimming pool just off the first fairway, half-way between Granny Clark's Wynd and the Swilcan Burn.

As far as the playing of golf goes at British and Irish clubs – and it is rare that facilities for other games are also available – this same absence of frills obtains. Players carry their bags over the shoulder or trundle them along on a trolley. Hardly anyone except visiting Americans takes a caddie. Indeed, at many courses, caddies have just about died out, and the only way you can be sure of getting one is to order one in advance.

Because the climate in the British Isles avoids the extremes we get in most sections of the United States, it takes fewer workmen and much less money to maintain a golf course in good condition, but it should also be mentioned that the golfers in those countries are not brought up to expect their courses to be manicured as fastidiously as they are over here.

Put this all together and you can see why a member of a first-rate club outside a large British city – say, Sunningdale or Wentworth in the London area – is required to pay annual dues of only $125 or thereabouts. His initiation fee would come to about the same amount.

Since we have been speaking of clubhouse monies and mores, this is probably the appropriate place to go into the recent changes in our way of life *outside* the clubhouse – changes that have to do with the way American golfers approach the game and play it. A good many of these changes strike me as unfortunate and unqualifiedly injurious to the fine fabric of golf, and while I grant you that I may feel this way because I am growing old and may deplore change *ipso facto*, I must say that I am not entirely convinced of this.

I think that everyone must agree that the biggest single problem in American golf today is the curse of slow play. During the weekend crush it is still possible at some clubs to get around the 18 holes in four hours or four hours and a quarter, but at most clubs the day of the five-hour round and worse has arrived. There is little question as to what has been the principal cause of this deplorable state of affairs: the average golfer, having watched the professional stars taking forever to play their shots on the tournament telecasts, now emulates his heroes in the mistaken belief that if he goes through the same lengthy productions they do, he will get the same results they do.

We have experienced the torture of being stuck for hours behind a foursome of exquisitely mediocre golfers (90-shooters or worse) who have somehow bought the fantasy that they are Nicklaus, Palmer, Trevino and Casper all in one, and who have all of the mannerisms (and some of the haberdashery) to prove it. From tee to green they cerebrate and ceremonialise over each shot as if the winning and losing of the Ryder Cup depended on it, but it is on the green that this maddening impersonation reaches its apex: they mark their ball just as professionally as the pros, and use up just as much time studying the line from all the angles, taking their practice strokes, getting down over the ball, getting up again to recheck the line, and so on and so forth.

This ritual is repeated without abbreviation over every putt; no one, apparently, ever concedes anyone else even a tap-in. More often than not, these foursomes act as if they own the course – they couldn't care less that they are holding up the whole parade. Without a doubt, the inordinate length of time it now takes to play a round of golf is one of the main reasons for the sensational rise in popularity that tennis is currently enjoying. In an hour and a half you can play three sets of tennis, or close to it. After that same amount of time, you're lucky to be on the sixth hole.

BILLY CASPER – *summoned for a practice session by King Hassan II of Morocco within two weeks of surviving a palace uprising.*

It is common for golfers who are criticised for slow play to remonstrate that the best players take time to concentrate carefully on every shot and that they intend to do so, too. This is an entirely irrelevant argument. Summoning your best concentration when you are over the ball is not one of the delinquencies that contribute to slow play. Where most golfers fall down is in not being ready to play when it is their turn. Only then do they start to do the things they should have done earlier, such as get to their ball, study their shot, settle on a club, get the feel of that club, and prepare to move into position to play the shot. Having made so many complimentary remarks about British and Irish golf, I am loath to throw any more roses that way, but the people over there certainly play golf at a good clip. The average foursome takes about three hours and a quarter for a round, and frequently less. I remember once playing Portmarnock in three hours flat, the second nine in a fivesome since Joe Carr was kind enough to join us on the 10th at the end of his working day. (A fivesome was possible since it was a weekday and there was no one on the course.) We didn't hurry that afternoon. We just didn't dawdle. That's how they go at it over there.

Golf cars are now in use on thousands of our courses, and you would imagine that this would help to speed things up. But the golf car, as I think we all appreciate, is a major problem in itself, both a boon and a bother. Some clubs have tried to limit the number of cars, and others have tried to ban them completely, but for better or for worse, the golf car is here to stay, a permanent part of the American golf scene. The latest figure I have on the total number of electric and gas golf cars in the United States is 240,000, which may possibly add up to more motorised transport than they have in Paraquay and Bolivia

combined. It is solemnly to be hoped that this fleet will prove to be a force for faster golf, especially since there are several obvious drawbacks to golf-car golf:

1. It robs you of the healthful exercise of a pleasant walk over rolling terrain.
2. It impairs the texture of golf. (If you are like me, you find that most golfers drive too fast and that you spend all your time during the ride not thinking of your golf but just hanging on. After he dumps you off, you have no feel of your distance from the green or how the hole is playing.)
3. It disturbs the proper tempo of golf. (There are times, for example, when every golfer wants a few moments alone so that he can collect himself after a rotten shot, a three-putt green or something equally upsetting. Golf-car golf simply doesn't give you enough time to brood.)

When all is said and done, the golf car is here to stay for two very good reasons. First, the rental of cars is a source of considerable income for golf clubs. Second, the caddie is dying out in many sections of the country. Boys can make more money these days doing other things, or they just don't want to caddie, period, and so an important institution is passing. Unlike in Britain where caddies customarily have been grown men, grizzled old-timers who seldom worked for long at any other job, in America young boys have always done the bulk of the carrying.

They started at it when they were 10 or so, or whenever they were big enough to carry a "ladies' bag", and often they continued on until they were out of high school. Primarily, they caddied because there weren't many other ways a kid could earn money – yet there was more to it than that. They enjoyed the ambience of the golf club and they liked the game of golf. A large number of them became low-handicap players and quite a few became champions, among them Francis Ouimet, Walter Hagen, Gene Sarazen, Chick Evans, George Von Elm, Johnny Farrell, the Turnesa brothers, Sam Snead, Byron Nelson and Ben Hogan.

In the American character there has always been a strong streak of idealism, and the young caddie brought this out. From the outset, individuals and groups set out to do something for the kids in the caddie yard. As early as 1907, two settlement-house workers in Boston, Robert A. Woods and John P. Whitman, conceived the idea of the summer caddie camp. It took boys from under-privileged families out of the slums and, in exchange for their services, they got to spend a summer in sunlight, fresh air and a generally nourishing atmosphere. In 1914, the Hinsdale Golf Club outside Chicago opened a playground and library which the caddies could use while waiting to go out. In the same year, Alexander H. Revell, a leader in the movement, saw to it that a new building was put up at the Chicago Golf Club in which there were lockers for the caddies and a washroom; adjacent to the building was a baseball diamond, gymnastic apparatus and a putting green.

And so it went. Golf opened the eyes of many young boys to a broader vista of life, and frequently it introduced them to men who took an interest in them and helped them.

Along with the caddie, another man who added immeasurably to the spirit and the fibre of American golf is on the verge of dying out: the transplanted Scottish pro. In the last decade of the 19th century, when golf was taking hold here, and, in a lesser way, down

through the first quarter of this century, there was a great demand for qualified teachers. It was the chance of a lifetime for any Scot who could break 85 and tell you to take the club back slowly, keep your head down, etc., etc. They poured into America – the Dunns, the Campbells, the Foulises, the Smiths, the McAndrewses, the Andersons, the Herds, the Nichollses, the Auchterlonies, the Lows, the MacDonalds, the Mackies, the Rosses, the Maidens, the Robertsons, the Thomsons, etc. Along with them came scores of English professionals and a few Irish and Welsh professionals, for there were jobs aplenty and, for a long while, no home-grown teachers of reputation to fill them. It wasn't until the 1920s, when our tournament golfers, led by Hagen and Jones, had overhauled the British and established themselves as the best players in the world, that the average American hacker would entrust his priceless, carefully burnished swing to an American-born teaching pro.

Whatever the reason, there is usually a very good chemistry between Scots and Americans, and the horde of pros who emigrated from North Berwick and Carnoustie and St. Andrews and Prestwick and beautiful downtown Auchtermuchty flourished. They loved the States, and we in turn loved everything about them: their enthusiasm, their politeness, their way of speaking, their friendliness, their independence, their humour, their honesty and, last but not least, their passion for golf. Scottish pros varied with the individual, of course. Some, like Jock Hutchison, were incessant talkers and story-tellers – and darn good ones. Others, like Freddie McLeod, whose basic mood was a sort of benevolent grumpiness, took a little longer to know. All of them, nevertheless, shared a number of traits in common. They were a breed, and a memorable one. They infused the game of golf with vitality, a sense of sport and the aura of tradition. They transmitted their engrossment with golfing technique, and they were devoted to their pupils. And they made the pro shop a wonderfully cheerful place to gather and chat, particularly if you purchased a golf ball or a package of tees there from time to time.

Maybe golf would have caught on just as successfully in America without the Scots and the other transplanted pros, but I rather doubt it. I doubt it most surely whenever I walk into one of our ultra-modern pro shops where three-fourths of the space is given over to Technicolor clothing piled in high cliffs on every side, a perfect reflection of the values of the resident pro who decided long ago that golf was okay but that the name of the game was money, and who has now gone 11 years without giving a lesson personally or working on his own game because a man can't be expected to be in two places at one time – at the cash register and out on the course.

For another thing, there has been a decline in golf etiquette. (I was going to say "sportsmanship", but that isn't the right word – not that "etiquette" is, really.) Golfers simply aren't as considerate nowadays as they should be of their fellow golfers. I don't know what has caused this, but I have an idea that (like slow play) it is to a large extent a reaction to studying the pros on television. Consciously or not, a lot of our players have become so intent on being as calm as Boros or as quietly determined as Casper that they couldn't care less what the other fellows in their foursome are up to.

In their self-absorption, they seldom bother to watch the other fellows' shots, so they can't help them find a ball if it ends up in trouble. They frequently play out of turn, and it is nothing for them to be moving or practice-swinging when another golfer is shooting. They would never dream of letting a faster group play through. They make too much noise on the course, and they are not above littering it. When they are playing a match, their approach is mordantly grim, and winning means too much to them. A friend of mine attributes this decrease in good manners to a majority of the members at many clubs today being men who started golf on public courses after World War II and have never moved past the code of every-man-for-himself that one picks up on overcrowded courses. Possibly. It might also be nothing more than a particularly conspicuous manifestation of the massive selfishness that has grown up in our country in the last 25 years.

We also tend today to put too much emphasis on scoring, as if that is all there is to golf, and not enough emphasis on playing good shots. This is reflected in the way we have softened up our courses by taking all the terror out of the rough, making our bunkers shallower and removing the overhanging lips, watering the greens so copiously, and other such measures. Like all the games that have lasted, golf is a test of skill, and when you reduce the amount of skill needed to play it well, you diminish not only its fascination but the pleasure and the sense of accomplishment it can give players of all degrees of proficiency. (On the other hand, I think it is absolutely right to do away with the rough in front of the tee, fairway bunkers within 150 yards of the tee, and other such hazards that come into play only for the high-handicap golfer, who has enough trouble without them.)

The authentic amateur is a rare bird. It is a matter of economics. Golf at the tournament level requires regular and intensive practice, not to mention a top priority on a man's thoughts and emotions over long stretches.

To be in a position to give it that much time and attention, it helps a lot if you happen to be fairly well-to-do, and from the beginning a high proportion of our stand-out amateurs have been. (Walter Travis, Bob Gardner, Jerry Travers, Bob Jones, Charley Yates, Dick Chapman, Frank Stranahan, and Bill Campbell are a few who come quickly to mind.) Of course, whenever a young fellow demonstrates that he can really play golf, it has never been difficult for him to latch on to a job with an insurance firm or a brokerage house or something along those lines which makes it possible for him to combine business and golf by playing "customer golf". It is often the only solution for the golfer of tournament class who doesn't want to become a professional.

And yet, everything taken into account, it is important for golf to have a goodly number of true amateurs of pronounced ability – men like Billy Joe Patton, Dr. Ed Updegraff, Charlie Coe, Bill Hyndman, Mike Bonallack, and Bill Campbell – who play the game purely and simply because they are crazy about it and because it enriches their lives. It is important, for when a game reaches the stage of commercialisation that golf has today under the goad of aggressive promoters and managers, it can develop dry rot. It is the amateurs who serve to remind us that golf can be an end in itself, that underneath the tinsel it is what we claim it to be – a great game.

I mention all this because, for some years now, the amateur spirit has been going out of golf at a dangerous clip. Above the level of the state championship the amateur game in this country is dominated today by college golfers who are attending school on scholarships – golf scholarships – in frank preparation for a career in professional golf.

The young men themselves are hardly to blame. When there is so much money and prestige in professional golf, you can understand why a promising young player wants to head in that direction. And when the game is being hustled by so many college administrators who regard it as a nonpareil promotional device, you can understand why a promising young player is delighted to accept a scholarship in return for hitting them long and straight for the old University of Sunshine. This pattern, however, emaciates amateur golf. The young men rarely stay amateur long enough for the amateur game to benefit from their presence.

Some of the facts about present-day collegiate golf are astounding – these, for example:

The number of American colleges that have golf teams has just about doubled in the last 15 years. Today close to 1,000 colleges do.

Quite a few colleges (including Nebraska, Arizona State and East Kentucky) award as many as eight golf scholarships each year. Texas and Memphis State give out eight to 10 golf scholarships each year, and Texas A. & M. gives out 12 to 14. That is high. At most "golf colleges", the average would be about two or three scholarships each year.

A good percentage of the scholarships are for small or moderate amounts, hovering in the neighbourhood of $500. The range is wide, however. At some colleges (such as Michigan, Wake Forest, and Southern Illinois), a golf scholarship can go as high as $3,000. At a few schools (including Southern Cal, Florida, Stanford, and Pennsylvania), it can be even more lucrative.

Has the whole college golf set-up become too monolithic, pressuring, and dollar-oriented? I think it has, and this is a point I have no choice but to enlarge upon whenever I get into one of those discussions in which, having criticised the present golf scholarship system, I find that old, reliable guaranteed-to-make-you-look-bad argument thrown at me: "Do you want to deprive some young man of a chance for a college education?" My answer is "Yes", unless he seriously means to try to get an education in college. I am not against golf scholarships or any kind of athletic scholarships – in fact, I am for them – as long as the young men involved have to meet the same academic requirements as everyone else to get into college and to stay in. Being old-fashioned enough to think that one of the principal aims of college is to teach a young man a sound sense of values, I must admit that I am a little disturbed by a system that teaches him to think first, and sometimes exclusively, in terms of money. I have met many young men on golf scholarships who are first-class fellows, but I have also met a considerable number who look upon college as a straight financial deal: the college gets their services for four years, and in return they get four years in which to prepare themselves for the professional tour.

In any event, the over-emphasis on college golf has resulted in a new breed of amateur, the pre-pro. I would suppose that the best working definition of an amateur is a fellow who devotes the bulk of his time to something else other than his golf, or whatever is his game or hobby. Some of the pre-pros, however, play golf practically every day of the year – more than the pros themselves do. That gives them great sharpness and makes it almost impossible for the "bourgeois" amateur to stay with them in competition, though perhaps the college golfers would dominate the amateur tournaments anyhow on competence alone. They certainly can play!

It would be amazing, really, if certain values were not lost when a sport has enjoyed an age as golden (in both senses of the word) as golf has in the last quarter of a century. Just think of this: where the national television networks carried a total of only five and a half hours of tournament golf in 1956, last year they carried over 100 hours. (Over 25 million viewers, a record number, watched the telecast of the final round of the 1971 Bing Crosby tournament, which, it should be noted, had the benefit of following the telecast of the Super Bowl.) Or think of this: during a six-week stretch last summer, the prize-money in the six tour tournaments added up to $1,115,000. (This is all the more incredible when you remember that it was not until 1958 that the *whole* tour – all 39 events played that year – first broke the million-dollar barrier in prize-money.)

With professional golf such a bedazzling plexus of riches, glamour, fame, and influence, the wonder is that the game has held its balance as well as it has. A good deal of the credit here goes to the two commanding champions of the last dozen years, Arnold Palmer and Jack Nicklaus. Despite all the fuss that has been made over him, Arnold has kept his head and his perspective as few men could have. He has always accepted such tiring, time-consuming jobs as shaking hands and signing autographs as part of the responsibilities of his position, and he performs them with peerless grace. Through it all, his love of golf has remained remarkably unimpaired. So has Nicklaus's. No other leader in any sport gives as much of himself to knowledgeable fans as Jack does, and during a tournament no one gives as much of himself to the Press as he does, or talks with such zest and humour and technical clarity. Golf has always been exceedingly lucky in the type of men who have been its champions.

14 Planned Practice Pays

The practice area is the most valuable plot of land to an aspiring golfer, and practice sessions are the most important single phase of the sport. Yet how many club golfers follow the good example set by tournament professionals? Precious few.

Most club members will have played for a considerable time, yet with only slight improvement in standards, while others who have allotted some time to practice sessions, or lessons, have been well rewarded by seeing their game rise to levels they had not thought possible.

One serious drawback is the time consumed, but with the majority of club golfers there is usually vast room for improvement and therefore any work or effort put in on the practice ground is almost bound to produce quick results.

But you must work along the right lines.

In 45 minutes you can hit twice the number of shots you would ordinarily need from tee to green during a normal round, and every shot can be repeated until you feel "safe" with it. But you must use practice time wisely. In fact you should plot it carefully.

Few golfers with a high or middle handicap are ever able to "cure" themselves and it is essential to have lessons from the golf club professional when there is a basic swing fault involved. After all he has the know-how, and he can *see* you in action which is something the golfer can never do himself.

The club professional can give you sound basic instruction, a routine which will cut out the major game-wrecking faults, and once such routine is given it must be adhered to. Treat his advice with indifference and the exercise is wasted, so once the practice pattern is plotted, stick to it. Practise only good points. Don't fall into the error of practising faults.

Start off easily with a few exercises to get the hands and wrists working before hitting a ball, and it is advisable to start by using an eight-iron, a nine-iron or a wedge.

The body will not be ready for the big effort of hitting long shots, so it must be loosened up with a series of little shots. Concentrate on a target. Don't just hit shots aimlessly. You can get careless that way. Train yourself with every shot and you take the habit on to the course.

Make sure with every shot that the stance is correct and that you are properly lined up.

Remember the nine-iron and wedge are valuable clubs these days and necessary for low scores, so put in 10 minutes hitting all types of shots – over hazards with a high loft, low shots, a full swing, three-quarter swing – from open, closed or square stance.

Practice gives you the chance to try out all that you may have learned from reading and watching, but it is fatal to experiment on the

Dividends

course! So after the warming-up phase, turn to the other clubs. Take your time. Hit every ball with considered purpose, and as before, aim for a target.

After all you are not on the practice ground to see how many balls you can hit in a given time. You do not do it at speed, or you should not do so, on the course, so why do it on the practice ground?

Become DELIBERATE. A good golfing word that, and it has 10 letters. We might all improve perhaps if, before making a shot, we counted up to 10.

John Jacobs is quoted as saying there are three aides to the business of improving golf in practice . . . the physical, the mental and the moral. Mental and moral are by far the most important.

On the mental plane you must have clarity, a clear picture of your plan, aims and objectives. From the moral point of view you get nowhere without conviction that you are on the right lines. In other words, wherever you get the pattern upon which you are working, you need to have faith in it.

Unless retired or semi-retired every golfer has to squeeze in practice time. He must be wise. Necessity for concentration has been stressed. Necessity for a plan of action and the taking of professional advice has been stressed. Now seclusion must also be emphasised.

Often a practice area is a meeting-place for friends, most of whom are always eager to offer bits of advice (every club has them!), to tell you what you are doing wrong, and how to make corrections.

Be firm. Ignore them. Listen to one word and you are well and truly sunk. You have been to the club professional. He has seen you and advised you. You have paid him, so heed him. It's as simple as that, it being far better to have one man teach you, who knows you, knows your game, and is always there when things go wrong. And he'll be watching you on the course to see you don't lapse into bad habits.

JACK NICKLAUS is by no means the biggest player on the professional golf tour, yet he is consistently the longest and straightest hitter in the world. His power comes from

a complete wind-up of the upper half of the body against firm resistance from feet and legs. The take-away from the ball is wide and low to the ground to ensure a full arc.

Although the club-head never goes past the horizontal position, Nicklaus pushes his hands high in the backswing to give the widest possible swing arc. Turning his left

foot out towards the target at address helps to clear the hips early in the downswing, making it easy for hands and arms to swing wide and free through ball at impact.

The real secret of Nicklaus's tremendous power is the perfect co-ordination of hands and body. If the hands whip into the ball ahead of the full body power, most of the energy generated is lost. Similarly, if the hands lag

behind the body at impact, the result is a weak downward chop into the ball. If the hips and body are moving correctly into the impact area, the hands cannot be used too early in the downswing.

16 Is Golf too Serious?

George Houghton

Yes. A symposium of tensions is taking over and threatening to change our laughter to tears.

Self-analysis, theories, high-powered techniques and television imagery are making us too performance-conscious. We are less inclined to go up to the ball and have a glorious go. We are now so sad and timid that anyone would think that Peter at the Pearly Gates chalks one up against us every time we fluff it!

In short, what used to be the joyous game of golf is now worrying us to death.

I take credit for first using the phrase "golf's emotion traffic". Now, I don't mind going on record as stating that this traffic is taking the wrong turning. Fun from the game in ratio to the ever increasing number of participants is down, down, down.

This has nothing to do with keenness. Golfers still sacrifice their careers by taking days off; wives, sick of neglect, still run off with chess players, or chaps who mow the lawn. . . . In drenching rain, we still risk pneumonia. Every weekend is a dance of death, but now it is not a happy death. Carefree abandon is on the way out.

Say what you like, golf is not the fun it was.

To make comparisons, one needn't go back to the 16th century when old Earl Cassilis played the Abbot of Crossraquel for the Abbot's *nose*, after they had downed a quart of port. Even yesterday's golfing high jinks are quite foreign to the sombre seventies.

The trouble nowadays is that we all have too much know-how. Every aspect of what was once a light-hearted game is carefully studied. We even try to out-dress the other guy!

I suppose everyone gets pleasure in a different way. Like women who only enjoy films that make them cry, golf addicts in the seventies want their "fix" of tensions. But do they have fun?

"We are not among the adrenaline cases because in Scotland we still consider golf to be a game for fun," said Gordon Durward, pro at Longniddry, when I asked him why, although Scotland has more golfers *per capita* than any country in the world, these days they never produce international champions.

Even in Scotland, certain jollities are slipping out of golf. Until fairly recently, the Brora club, in Sutherland, always had an annual captain versus vice-captain all-night match (about 30 a side) starting at 10 p.m. and finishing with breakfast.

A great night game – just for fun – was held in 1928 at St. Andrews, when Angus Hambro organised illuminated golf on the 1st and 18th to celebrate his captaincy. Mostly the light came from cars in Links Place, or lanterns, but also regular rockets added to the gaiety. I suppose this kind of frivolity would be like playing crown and anchor in the parish kirk these days.

Alas, there is very little skylarking in the sombre seventies. How seldom does one hear, for example, of those wonderful cross-country golf record-breakers? Like Tommy Ovier, who, having lived glorious golf until he was 91, passed gently away in 1941 while reminiscing about the 35 miles cross-country Maidstone to Littlestone game he played in 1,087 shots, having lost 17 balls, and seven caddies. This feat won Tommy a wager of £5, but he said at the time he would have paid out a fiver for the fun.

C. A. Macey, pro at Crowborough, did 12 consecutive rounds in 1944 at Folkestone – while shells from long-range German guns were landing on the course!

These sort of larks were regular occurrences in the cheery golf scene a quarter of a

continued on page 129

ERIC BROWN *dominated Scottish golf for more than 20 years. Unbeaten in Ryder Cup singles matches against America. Twice Ryder Cup captain.*

BERNARD GALLACHER *(left)*, *first of the new breed of young Scottish super-stars.*

LU LIANG HUAN, *known universally as Mr. Lu since his second place behind Lee Trevino in the 1971 Open at Birkdale.*

JOHN MILLER, *one of the exciting young stars of the American circuit. Finished eighth in the 1966 U.S. Open as an amateur and second behind Nicklaus last year in the U.S. Masters.*

NEIL COLES *(right) Britain's most successful and most consistent professional. Has three times been top money-winner and twice winner of the Harry Vardon Trophy as leader in the Order of Merit.*

CHRISTY O'CONNOR *(left) who has finished in the top 25 in the Open Championship eight times in the past 10 years. Won £25,000 in the 1970 John Player Classic.*

BRIAN HUGGETT, *winner of 16 major tournaments since 1962 and one of Britain's most consistent professionals. Winner of the Harry Vardon Trophy in 1968.*

TOM WEISKOPF, *winner of over half a million dollars in his six completed years on the American circuit. Winner of the Kemper and Philadelphia events in 1971.*

century ago. Not so now. I cannot see the keener-than-mustard tycoon pros of today finding time for the lighter side of golf, although once in a while good humour flickers through.

Winnie Palmer is quoted: "Nothing in life gives Arnold so much fun as golf. Even in 1959, when he lost three big tournaments by missing putts less than the length of a table he still came home each time bubbling with the fun of it." Of course, that was years ago. Arnold does his share of scowling in the seventies.

Of the professionals, Walter Hagen probably got more amusement from golf than any, before or since. Only once did I see him play, in 1928 at St. Cloud, when he was beaten 8 and 7 by Aubrey Boomer. Hagen had angered the crowd (briefly) because he arrived more than an hour late, straight from the night spots of Montmartre. After the match, he went to England where Archie Compston beat him 18 with 17 to play in the 36-holes match at Moor Park. Everyone knows of this disgraceful encounter. The frolicking Hagen, giving the crowd full entertainment value, played in a red schoolboy cap which he had borrowed from someone in the crowd! A month later, just for fun at Sandwich, he won the British Open.

I don't suppose it really matters that nowadays tournament strain produces more grumbles and ulcers among top pros than ever before. After all, there are 10 or 12 million golfers in the world, and the tournament pros probably don't number more than a couple of thousand. The trouble is that tension-torn souls like Nicklaus, Player and Jacklin, set the pattern that armies of formerly carefree golfers attempt to copy.

All the way to the bank tournament players sing "I'm ill with the pressures." This is their theme song, and what worries me is that thousands of golfers are joining in the chorus and grumbling about missed putts when they should be galloping to the next tee for the sheer pleasure of swinging with joyous abandon.

Instead of bringing gladness, golf nowadays seems to make folk angry, usually at themselves. American cartoonist Don Herold wrote: "You can't play good golf when you are mad at golf. You can't play good golf when you are mad at anything, or anybody. . . . You've got to be at peace with the universe. That's a big order. But golf's a big order, and the fun's worth it. Maybe, golf is the best reason you ever had to calm down."

Hillbilly Sam Snead says to "get peaceful" he talks to his ball. "This isn't going to hurt," he says, "Sambo is just going to give you a nice little ride. You're sitting up fat and ready. Let's have some fun. . . ."

I think most golfers *know* that golf *should* be fun, but these days so many of us are losing out because we fret. All this is symptomatic of the hectic computerised times in which we live. Persuaders, with a capital "P" (you all know who I mean) are urging golf into what big business calls the rat race. We should oppose this and hold on to the good old-fashioned kind that drives away dull care.

There are, of course, pockets of resistance (like me, and I hope you) to all this dead serious stuff. Some of us still start with a song in our hearts, to enjoy uninhibited golf, shorn of technical jargon, but chock-a-block with "needle", without which the fun is incomplete.

The Golf Addicts Society of Britain keeps the fun flag flying. We go away for an annual week – two rounds a day – and anyone who plays to his handicap is ostracised. If a member says anything comparable to "I'm not following through," or "If only I could pivot," he has to pay a round of drinks. We're

trying to cut out the patter, and just enjoy the golf.

Unfortunately, the anguish variety – where every putt over a foot must be slotted, and the winner comes in pale with strain and makes for the lav where he is slightly sick – becomes more prevalent. So many golfers in the seventies burn with self-hatred every time they make an imperfect shot. These days, we are mostly like that. We don't all get facial ticks and nervous stammers, but neither do we get maximum fun from our golf.

To our eternal shame we are all pumping too much science into the game. Hungry for "secrets", we read too much, and listen to too many hints. We are as self-analytical as nuns taking the veil.

The competitive side of golf is no fiercer now than it has always been, but today this aspect is less healthy, because there is more internal conflict. In mental turmoil we castigate ourselves because we are swinging too fast, not holding on.... Putting pitifully, and so on. As golfers, we are putrid. We hate ourselves.

It is gratifying that some people try to preserve the fun contained in golf. Some years ago, Professor O. S. Sinnatt, while in charge of aeronautical sciences at Cranwell, invented a golf ball that would neither slice nor pull. The North British Rubber Co. was advised against manufacturing by the R. and A. The ball, it seemed, could not be hit so far because part of the go-forward power was used up in producing rotational energy by the exertion of the gyroscopic torque necessary to keep the sliced ball on a direct path....

Hitting a long drive is exciting and we would not want that to be eliminated. Nevertheless, I like to think that the authority deciding against the ever-straight ball decreed that way because *banana shots are such fun*.

"Thank God we still have the President's Putter," said a golf buddy to me recently. He was deploring certain manifestations of the past few decades that we both consider detrimental to golf.

The annual contest 'twixt university golfers of Oxford and Cambridge is always held in rare defiance of mid-winter weather, and the choice of January for this important fixture can perhaps be considered a caprice. Often there is snow, and usually rain, but cancellation is never considered. When a journalist asked why another date later in the year with more reliable weather was not chosen, he got a simple answer. "Because members of this society like to play our tournament in January. Inclement weather adds to the fun."

These days, this kind of attitude is heartening, but rare. Golf becomes increasingly inhibited. Jollity perishes among the laughless masks. Soon there will be only dead-keen players with dead-pan expressions.

Tigers and rabbits, amateurs and pros, rush along the tension trail, jittery with anxiety neurosis. Having noted the following in the *Daily Mail*, May 31, 1972, is there any wonder?

"In an argument over a playing permit, a guard at a municipal course in Buffalo handcuffed and beat a golfer with his club, then took out his gun and shot him dead."

scoring in stroke-play. In no uncertain terms, the rule says that score-cards must be scrupulously filled in, audited and counter-signed. During a 1970 professional tournament a player accidentally put down the total for the first nine holes in the space on the card intended for hole 9. It had to count, and the checking authority credited the player with 33 strokes more than he had played.

The penultimate item in Rule 41 shows that the R. and A. will stand for no nonsense. It is the law that penalises you if you help your partner (or opponent). I suppose this would cover the case of dear old Bobby Fox at the Hertfordshire club whose foursomes partner was always telling him to fasten his shoe-laces!

Penalties are slapped down pretty hard.

Detailed and severe rules and regulations are necessary for competitions, tournaments and cash contests, when no holds are barred. But for the splendid day-to-day golf, I reckon you could print all the commandments you need on a bus ticket.

WATCH YOUR MANNERS, AND DON'T CHEAT.

ERIC BROWN – *winner of the Scottish Professional Championship eight times. With* JOHN PANTON *he dominated Scottish golf for 20 years.*

17 Scotland will Produce more Champions Raymond Jacobs

Like a schoolmaster distributing examination papers to a trembling pupil and then retreating to the comfortable and all-knowing isolation of his invigilating desk, the editor pulled the pin from this grenade of a subject, lobbed it over to me and then withdrew to a safe distance, to duck his head beneath the top of the trench and await results.

For nothing is so aggravating to the observer of the Scottish golfing scene as to be asked why for so long so few of the breed have become champions outside their own country. And, moreover, nothing is better calculated to reduce the Scottish brain to the consistency of porridge than trying to advance rational explanations for this unbalanced state of affairs without making them sound perilously like special pleading.

There has been, so far as I know, no cogent reason why Scotland, with no great history or tradition in the world of Grand Prix motor-car racing nor widespread opportunities to indulge in that expensive sport, should have produced within a decade two world champions in Jim Clark and Jackie Stewart. Maybe that dual achievement can be classed as so untypical as to deserve being reduced to the ranks of coincidence. It did happen, however.

Meanwhile, there are recurring manifestations of Scotland's inability, despite having a large golfing population who enjoy unparalleled opportunities for playing the game, to extend success as individuals beyond the borders. The Amateur Championship is a strong case in point. Every now and then a quartet of Scotsmen reach the quarter-final round, whereupon up pop the headlines in the morning papers, as predictably as the symbols of a cash register, "Four Scots in the Last Eight." Almost as certainly the next set of headlines read, "No Scots in the Last Four."

It is an incontrovertible fact that not for 15 years has a Scot, since Reid Jack, won the Amateur Championship and one has done so only five times since its resumption after the First World War. Nor, for that matter, has a Scotswoman won the British title for 14 years. As for the Open Championship, if Jock Hutchison and Tommy Armour, who were naturalised Americans by the time they won in 1921 and 10 years later respectively, are excluded one has to go back to George Duncan, in 1920, to arrive at the name of the last Scot to capture the title. The victory in 1893 of Willie Auchterlonie, the last Scottish champion actually resident in the country, is now almost lost in the mists of time.

Making every allowance for Scotland's lack of population and the spread of the game to other countries better endowed financially, in numbers, climate, the right facilities and – perhaps most significantly – attitude, this has been a notably dismal performance from a nation who, as long ago as the 15th century, had to be reprimanded by Act of Parliament for indulging in golf and football to the detriment of practising archery, then the recognised method of Sassenach-bashing.

To be sure, there have been occasional near-misses – but very occasional. If Eric Brown had not taken six at the 72nd hole at Royal Lytham in 1958 he could at least have been involved in the play-off in which Peter Thomson defeated Dave Thomas, and that is the last recorded instance of a Scottish professional being in true contention for the title. Leslie Taylor, Jimmy Walker and Ronnie Shade reached the final of the Amateur Championship, the only players to have done so since the last war apart from Reid Jack – but they were beaten.

This is the point at which it seems appropriate to zero in on the root causes of this rather extraordinary lack of success and then set out to try to show why in future years I

Scotland will Produce more Champions

For most of his playing career JOHN PANTON *shared with* ERIC BROWN *the national and international honours for Scotland. No younger players were able to push him aside until he was past his half-century.*

believe the pendulum will begin to swing, not before time, in the other direction. There is, after all, no effect without cause. Sceptics can stop here – sympathisers may read on.

First of all, for the first 20 years or so of both the Open and Amateur Championships the Scots largely had the field to themselves. They kept winning and established, one has to suspect, a pretty strong conceit of themselves, simply because there was scarcely any meaningful opposition. At that time was established a basic flaw in the Scottish golfing character; golf was a game to be played, practice was looked on as deviationism of the most suspicious kind – and besides, who would willingly stand on a practice tee, even assuming that such a facility was available, hitting shots in rain that fell like horizontal stair rods.

Scottish professionals began to sink almost without trace as valid competitors. Since the Second World War, who, with the exception of Eric Brown and John Panton, have been able to catch international as well as national attention until the very recent emergence of Bernard Gallacher, Ronnie Shade and Harry Bannerman? The amateurs have fared scarcely better over the last 40 years or so, during which time lasting individual impacts have been made beyond the Border by such few as Jack McLean, Hector Thomson, Alex Kyle, Reid Jack, Charlie Green and Shade.

Certainly the professional game is the one which catches most of the public interest. But the amateur side of affairs has a distinctive existence and, of course, it has increasingly become the training ground for players who have set their sights on crossing the great divide between the two camps. The importance, therefore, of recent developments in Scottish golf apply with roughly equal force to both sides; they have undoubtedly helped raise amateur standards (witness, for example, Scotland's excellent results in recent

years in international matches) and the benefits will, hopefully, be translated into professional golf by those who make it their career.

There is, regretfully, nothing anyone can do about the weather. Scottish golfers have always had to put up with its harsh behaviour and presumably they always will. The lack of adequate practice grounds is simply a relic of less organised days, when clubs were formed with the disarmingly naïve objective of giving the members the opportunity to play over a course. And there are now so many of these relative to the population – about 400 at the last count – that driving-range entrepreneurs like John Jacobs have said that to open one in Scotland would be an economic folly.

Another obstacle that has stood in the way of a faster development of Scottish golfing resources is the links course. They are a fine attraction for the tourist and, of course, the only outlet for many club golfers, but when the numbers who regularly play on seaside courses are related to the number of players of the highest class who have learned the game over them the ratio is almost non-existent. And the reason for that is that a specific technique for manœuvring the ball round a links in the wind has been evolved, whereby the ball is kept low and out of trouble with the flatter swing and stronger grip which is next to useless on inland courses.

I once, for instance, stood by the 12th tee at Ganton and watched a succession of Scottish women golfers trying to negotiate the tall trees guarding the corner of that dog-leg hole. Two of them, as I recall, had the method to give the ball sufficient distance and height through the air to carry those dominant obstacles; the rest had no chance of doing so, nor would they have

HARRY BANNERMAN (right) *made a late but rapid entry into Scotland's international field, distinguishing himself in his first Ryder Cup match at St. Louis in 1971.*

BERNARD GALLACHER (below) *and* (far right) *swept to the top of the British P.G.A. Order of Merit in 1969, bringing a hint of better things to come for Scottish golf.*

succeeded had they stood on that tee all day.

That illustration of a commonplace dilemma leads on to another fundamental lack in Scottish golf – the acute shortage, bordering on almost total starvation of inland courses where off the tee the ball has to be kept in the air – as distinct from relying on run – to gain distance and where second shots with long irons and even woods have to be played regularly to reach greens.

Most Scottish inland courses are too open – in other words, the more off-line a shot is hit in many instances the better is the chance of getting away with it. One simply "borrows" an adjacent fairway, and that is quite unlike the proposition which faces the player on one of the Berkshire or Surrey courses, where the fairways, tightly hemmed in by trees, offer no convenient escape route. (It is no accident that Scotland, never renowned for its wealth of accurate drivers, had one who was David Blair; he learned his golf on those southern courses, where the margin for error was minimal.)

The nearest approach to this type of course that exists in Scotland are at Blairgowrie and Downfield, Dundee, and I do not think it is any coincidence that in 1972 major professional tournaments were held at each for the first time with some success and that more tournaments are scheduled for both. The choice is certainly limited, but that these two courses are being used is a definite step in the right direction.

At the end of the day, however, the most important element in the making of a golfer – apart from temperament, which is born and cannot be taught, though it can be developed and disciplined – is the learning of a technique which will stand up under pressure. The signs are that, despite a basic lack of practice facilities and a shortage of properly qualified teachers, Scotland is beginning to acquire

137

A picture that epitomises the revival of Scottish golf: CHARLIE GREEN, *a veteran of international Scottish honours, congratulates the 1971 Scottish Amateur Champion,* SANDY STEPHEN, *at 17 years old his junior by 21 years.*

players who are better schooled than they have ever been. But, importantly, because players are individual and coaching recognises this central fact of golf, there is no danger of a nation of golfing machines being turned out, every ounce of natural ability having been wrung out of them by a slavish adherence to a particular method.

The present-day Scottish amateur increasingly looks, when he swings the club, as if he knows what he is doing. This is the product of the belief that players should learn more about the mechanics of the swing, especially their own, so that when it goes wrong they are, in the absence of immediate professional advice, able to put it right themselves.

It is on this basis that I believe Scottish golfers will gradually come to give a better account of themselves internationally in the

years immediately ahead. In the last two years we have seen Sandy Stephen, aged 17, and David Robertson, aged 14, capturing the Scottish Amateur and Boys' titles respectively, both the youngest to do so, and Scottish teams winning successive home international championships as well as showing up prominently in European championships. Taking into account the earlier maturing of young players nowadays, these achievements are, it seems to me, significant straws in the wind. I do not say that Scotland, more than any other country, will suddenly start to produce a stream of infant phenomena, but the indications are that a degree of hopeful pathfinding has been carried out that will have continuing repercussions in the years ahead.

Nor, since I am not a racing tipster, do I intend to nominate a selection of names most likely to succeed. To do so would imply a sort of time-table, which might have the effect of branding as failures anyone who did not keep within an arbitrary schedule, an unacceptable form of additional pressure on possible candidates for real advancement. After all, throughout the world, young golfers are progressing faster than they have ever done; it is worth recalling that Ben Hogan was almost 41 when, in 1953, he won the British and U.S. Opens and the Masters.

Sometimes, without any real justification, Scottish golfers have seemed to expect the worst to happen – a by-product, perhaps, of a lurching economy. If they can replace this unnecessary lack of self-confidence with a belief in themselves, at the same time as they are developing their skills, there does not seem to be any reason why Scotland should not produce more champions. The generations which have not known the continuing taste of failure should be better able to succeed.

ARNOLD PALMER takes a typically solid position even for a wedge shot. The feet, legs and hips are firmly planted, while the upper body remains active. This becomes clear

as Palmer goes into a controlled one-piece take-away, with legs and hips resisting and shoulders turning through a full 45° although the club-head has only moved a few feet.

Shoulders fully turned, hips and legs resisting as Palmer reaches the top of his backswing with the wedge. The hips start the downswing, leading the arms from their

horizontal position at the top into a free-wheeling hit
through the ball. Note how the right shoulder stays
back as the hands unleash the club-head into the ball.

Here is a lesson for every golfer. Palmer has cleared his hips to allow the hands and arms a clear path through the ball, but the hip movement has not been exaggerated.

His right hand crosses over his left in the follow-through.
A driving action through the ball will cause this cross-
over to occur later than with a wristy action.

19 The Rules of the Game

George Houghton

My friend Frantisek, born and bred in Prague, knows nothing of golf. So you might say we were starting from scratch. This is how I explained the game.

"Golf," I said, "is hitting a certain kind of ball into a certain kind of hole with a certain kind of stick. The fewest hits wins."

"Is that all?" asked Frantisek.

"Basically, yes" I said.

"And you play in a special uniform?"

"No," I said, "You wear what you like, and the golf course can be any size, anywhere."

I went on to explain "a green", adding that the area was indetermined, and the distance between hole and "teeing ground" was likewise unspecified. "All you have to do," I said, "is to count the number of hits required, and keep them to a minimum."

"How nice," said Frantisek. "A game so simple!"

Heaven knows what my young Czech friend will think if he is ever shown nearly 200 pages of small print at the beginning of *The Golfer's Handbook*.

Here we have the whole grisly works, beginning with the names of the 12 sound men and true (with their eight "auxiliaries" from foreign parts) whose job is to revise, delete and add rules as circumstances require. Additionally, points of etiquette are detailed; there is guidance on how the rules can be applied, a list of the game's governing bodies, an explanation of how the handicapping system works, and other items calculated to make your head spin, particularly if you start by thinking golf is a simple, uncomplicated game.

The aforesaid are incidentals. Most of this section of the comprehensive golf book is filled with the 41 Rules of Golf, laid down by the Royal and Ancient Golf Club of St. Andrews. They bear the seal of top authority.

After the rules, there is a list of suggestions

for more. This part is called Local Rules, and these can legitimately be added to the other governing laws by individual club officials who love to interfere by restricting play in bad weather, putting stretches of the course out of play, and that kind of thing.

The Honourable Company of Edinburgh Golfers, in their club-house at Muirfield, proudly display the first Rules of Golf which were originally drafted by officials of that club. In those days, before the game was complicated, there were only 13 commandments, and these were drawn up in 1744. Then, the R. and A. took over this department of the game, and began to show us that golf was not the lovely simple game it seemed. Other clubs have contributed additional material, like Rule 32 which gives a player relief when a "burrowing animal's" activities interfere with his ball. The rabbit nuisance seems first to have been noticed at Scotscraig, down the road from St. Andrews. That club had their own private regulation about the menace, and this rule was ultimately incorporated into the R. and A. Standard Rules.

This business of adding bits of legislation, seemingly, has gone on over the years. Apparently, although there are sometimes signs to the contrary, the R. and A. are anxious to please everyone. It would appear that any golfer who has been able to produce evidence of an incident that just *could* happen has framed a rule to cover the contingency, if it has not already been provided for.

This generous treatment of golf lawyers, the biggest bores at any club, must be wrong. Without much thought, one could contrive a dozen possibilities not covered by the Rules of Golf. Nor need they be.

In particular, I personally hate Rule 4 which categorically states that it is prohibited to waive rules. What nonsense! They really mean that players cannot cook up their own rules *in competitions, or tournaments*, but they don't say so. The ingenious improvements devised by regular four-balls must not be restricted. I know dozens of happy golf games that would not be so good if the players couldn't bend the rules.

For example: if one of the famous veteran Ironsides of Carnoustie finds his ball in a bunker he immediately changes it for an old one. Why should he risk damaging a nice new ball? Rule 33 says: "When a ball lies in or touches a hazard nothing shall be done which may in any way improve its lie. The player shall not touch the ground. . . . The ball may not be lifted for identification." There is no rule which says a player shall not change his ball in a bunker.

Rules will never cover everything that happens in golf. What about the case in the United States of the cameraman who started his movie camera whirring noisily whenever a particular player was putting or driving? This was calculated to worry the player, and no doubt did, probably to the financial gain of the cameraman. What golf rule could cover that?

Of course, the rules are only supposed to apply to participants, but what about the player with the noisy pipe? Gurgling dottle can be very off-putting. What rule takes care of that kind of thing? There is nothing.

On the other hand, Rule 37-3 says: "If a player infringe a Rule or Local Rule so as to *assist* his partner's play, the partner incurs the relative penalty in addition to any penalty incurred by the player." In other words, the rule is nullified. That bit of legislation, at any rate, appears to be unnecessary, particularly since the same point in precisely the same words is repeated in Rule 41.

Of course, it is easy enough to go through 41 rules and show how many of them need never apply. Also, it would be wickedly improper to accuse the Rules of Golf Committee of expanding their task to keep them in constant employment. After all, theirs is a labour of love, and we must give them credit for hoping that their rules will add to, not detract from, our enjoyment.

I think the main criticism (plugged for years by Henry Longhurst) is that the whole rules structure is too cumbersome. What we want is simplicity. An example of the contrary is Item 2 in Rule 17: "If a ball lie in long grass, rushes, bushes, whins, heather or the like, only so much thereof shall be touched as will enable the player to find and identify the ball. . . . *The player is not of necessity entitled to see the ball when playing a stroke.*"

The final sentence is intriguing, holding endless possibilities for fun.

That great character, "Brooks" Peckover Burrill, President of the Welsh Golfing Union, when umpiring a match was called upon to adjudicate on the correct procedure of play when a ball landed in soft cow-dung. "Lift without penalty," said Brooks, immediately, "a ball shall not be played in motion."

In the case mentioned, the decision was rather at variance (though justly so) to Rule 25 which contains: "When a ball is in water, the player may, without penalty, make a stroke at it while it is moving, but he must not delay to make his stroke *in order to allow the wind or current to better the position of the ball.*"

The italics are mine to draw attention to what one might consider unnecessary verbiage. Good heavens, if a golfer is keen, or ingenious enough to paddle for a shot, surely he should not be deprived of using wind or current to his advantage! This, it seems to me, is taking to extremes the business about getting help from an "outside agency".

Rule 27 decides that if the wind moves your ball on the green you take a penalty. I consider this very severe. Fortunately, there are always ploys to take care of these injustices. When the bright boys are playing in conditions when balls can be moved by the wind while being addressed on the green, instead of risking this happening, the player merely picks up his ball for cleaning, then replaces with a gentle press down. This anchors the ball, and a lick of spit helps.

Sometimes I am not happy about the general attitude of the Rules of Golf Committee. They seem to make the game more difficult, and this, of course, hardly ever increases the pleasure. Take the rule about the flag. We have to have it attended on the green, and removed when the ball approaches. Some of us preferred the old drill of leaving the flagstick to help the ball into the hole. Most of us need all the help available.

On one thing you can always count: committees stick together through thick and thin. Rule 36 goes into the question of these dictatorial bodies. "The Committee (meaning the individual club committee) has no power to waive a Rule of Golf", says the R. and A., then goes on to ease the blow by stating: "A penalty of disqualification, however, may in exceptional individual cases be waived or be modified or be imposed. . . . If the Committee consider such action warranted."

This streak of leniency frightens me whenever I think of Joe Corrin, Club Champion many times of the Castletown Club on the Isle of Man. Joe arrived late for his starting time in the President's Prize competition. Instead of ruling that he follow on at the end of the field, or be fitted in, a committeeman disqualified the unfortunate competitor. Heartbroken and angry, Joe left the club – and golf – for 10 years.

Some say that in all games and sports only in the Rules of Golf is there no margin for common sense. They quote Rule 38 about

STUART BROWN (U.K.)

A professional since 1965, he first attacked the circuit in 1970 and has since impressed the experts with steady consistency of performance. Won the Lusaka Dunlop Open in 1971 and same year tied for second place in the Penfold-Bournemouth tournament. Finishing 36th in the P.G.A. Order of Merit in his first year, he rose to 17th position in 1971.
Born August 11, 1946. Height 5 ft. 10½ in. Weight 12 st. 7 lb.

PETER BUTLER (U.K.)

In 13 years has won 15 major P.G.A. and overseas championships and been placed in the top 15 of the P.G.A. Order of Merit for the last 10 years. Represented Britain three times in Ryder Cup matches (1965, 1969 and 1971), he was also selected for England's winning team in the Double Diamond Home International in 1971. Won the Classic International at Copt Heath in 1971, was runner-up in the Benson and Hedges Golf Festival at Fulford, fifth in the Agfa-Gevaert tournament at Stoke Poges, third in the Martini International at Royal Norwich, fifth in Carrolls International, and finished seventh in the P.G.A. Order of Merit.
Born March 25, 1932. Height 6 ft. Weight 13st.

CLIVE CLARK (U.K.)

Following brilliant amateur career, turned professional in 1965 and registered first major success following year when taking the Danish Open. Tied for third place with Gary Player in the Open Championship, 1967 and that year finished third in the P.G.A. Order of Merit. Following short American trip returned to take the Agfa-color tournament, and later the Bowmaker tournament in 1968.
Born June 27, 1945. Height 5 ft. 11 in. Weight 11 st. 6 lb.

20
Ten of the World's Top Players

Billy Casper
Bob Charles
Neil Coles
Tony Jacklin
Jack Nicklaus
Peter Oosterhuis
Arnold Palmer
Gary Player
Lee Trevino
Peter Thomson

Plus a Portrait Gallery of the
100 Leading International Tournament
Stars

BILLY CASPER

After 18 years as a professional and with winnings of over £500,000 in America alone, where he has won 50 events of major importance, Casper believes his best years are yet to come!

Quiet, considerate and courteous off the course, he shows the same qualities in action and retains a degree of popularity in whichever event he enters. The year 1971 was not one of his best, he slipped from second to 10th in the U.S. money-winners list, but he maintained his record of at least one big win a year when lifting the Kaiser with rounds of 67–65–69–68.

Perhaps his biggest moments in such an outstanding career to date have been the success in 1959 and 1966, the years he won the U.S. Open. He won the Masters in 1970.

Born in California in 1931, he now resides at San Diego with his wife Shirley and seven children and has one real ambition – to win the British Open Championship, an event for which he has been favourite in previous years.

BOB CHARLES

Noted for his superb putting skill, Charles has amassed a considerable fortune in a quiet sort of way.

Never gimmicky, never making the sort of bizarre statements likely to make news, never boastful of his successes, this nice-to-know New Zealander has made many friends in all corners of the world.

To see him quietly and methodically put together an under-par round, or to approach a long putt and effortlessly stroke it down without the semblance of a smile crossing his deep-tanned features, is in itself a complete course in golf approach.

It was putting that brought him through to win the Piccadilly World Match-play Championship in 1969 when he beat G. Littler at the 37th hole.

Putting again, especially in the third round, helped him towards a second-place tie in the W. D. and H. O. Wills Open.

A previous winner of the British Open (1963) with 277, which has not been bettered since, Charles has a more than useful record in the States as well.

NEIL COLES

Neil Coles, known in some circles as "The Professor", gets through an enormous amount of golf during a year.

At the age of 38 he refuses to fly – yet if he lifted this self-imposed ban he might well double his income.

In the last two years alone he has scored nine major successes within Europe. In 1970 he chalked up five victories, the Italian Open and the Walworth-Aloyco on the Continent, the Sumrie Fourball tournament (along with Bernard Hunt), the Daks (his third success) and the Bowmaker. He finished so high in other events that he managed to top the £18,000 mark in winnings. Four more major tournaments were his in 1971, the Penfold-Bournemouth, Daks (shared with Brian Huggett), Carrolls International, and his first ever Open, the German title.

Twice winner of the Harry Vardon Trophy, three times top money-winner, Coles has been appearing more on the Continent in recent years and with telling effect, and although he is more inclined to favour home comforts as against "living out of a suitcase", such jaunts might well be extended.

A lot of people would like to see this unassuming and skilful professional at work.

TONY JACKLIN

The man who brought British golf to life when he won the Open Championships of Britain and America in 1969 and 1970, the first British holder of the U.S. crown since Ted Ray some 50 years before, Jacklin has become the number one crowd-puller in home events and just as popular during his American appearances.

A rare golfer, he has proved himself in many a tense situation, being able to concentrate and produce the right shot at the most critical moment. He appears to thrive on tension.

No doubt his early decision to tackle the U.S. circuits has had much to do with this attitude to the game. You have to be tough on the tour and Jacklin has shown he can be just that.

In fact he proved it within a few weeks of arriving in America in 1968 when he took the Greater Jacksonville Open. He came back and next year won the British Open Championship at Royal Lytham and St. Annes.

For his contribution to British golf Jacklin was honoured by the Queen with an O.B.E. and the P.G.A created him a life vice-president.

Married, with one son, he likes shooting, plays the occasional game of tennis or squash, and is determined to make the Grand Slam.

JACK NICKLAUS

What more can be said about Jack Nicklaus? Mere hard figures reveal that since turning professional in 1961 this hard-to-beat dedicated golfer has won over £500,000 in prizemoney on the American tour alone, and has never been outside the top four money-winners in any one year.

In that time 38 titles have come his way, plus two successes in the British Open Championship and a 2 and 1 win over Lee Trevino in the 1970 Piccadilly World Matchplay Championship.

One of golf's nicest people. Nicklaus has built up a large business complex to look after his varied interests, such as marketing, publicity, promotions and course designing.

Born in 1940 at Columbus, Ohio, educated Ohio State University, he was first prominent when winning the U.S. Amateur in 1959 and 1961 and following the latter success he decided to join the tour.

Now, with a fine home in Florida, four children ranging from three to 11, and wife Barbara, Nicklaus sits back, selects his targets and plans accordingly.

A formidable opponent indeed, he has, this year, equalled the late Bobby Jones's record of 13 championship victories, by winning the first half of the Grand Slam – the Masters and U.S. Open.

PETER OOSTERHUIS

The name most likely to be making news for the next decade. He is 24, married, a professional for four years and already picking up golf titles in much the same way as a kid with coconuts at a fairground.

A short, but brilliant, amateur record brought him international honours when at 19 he was a Walker Cup player, later being placed third in individual aggregates during the Eisenhower Trophy.

His first P.G.A. season saw him 17th in the Order of Merit, in 1970 he was seventh, and top in 1971 to win the Harry Vardon Trophy.

A remarkable start to what can only be a remarkable career.

In his first Ryder Cup début he scored singles victories over Arnold Palmer and Gene Littler. For the second successive year he was top in the South African Order of Merit. In 1970 his winnings were over the £10,000 mark, and again in 1971. His 1972 start suggests the pattern will continue.

He holds very firm opinions as to his own shortcomings, and once these are ironed out his intentions are to have a serious look at the U.S. possibilities.

ARNOLD PALMER

Born in Latrobe, Pennsylvania, in 1929, Palmer was in golf from his first day. Being the son of a golf professional-greenkeeper the golf course was his natural playground, and when no higher than a golf bag he was looking a good prospect.

A short spell at Wake College and another with the U.S. Coast Guard preceded his entry into the professional ranks in 1954.

Less than a year later, just married, he set out for Canada and captured the Canadian Open. The following year three more successes came his way and since then the total has become an impressive one, reaching well into the 60s.

This includes a double in the British Open (1961, 1962) and a like record in the Piccadilly World Match-play Championship when beating Neil Coles 2 and 1 in 1964, and Peter Thomson by 1 hole in 1967.

The strange thing is that one major title still evades him – the U.S. P.G.A. Championship. Having won well over £500,000 in his time, Palmer is a wealthy man with many outside interests (as well as owning a golf course!) and although he need never play for cash again, he will continue to chase that missing title – among others. Palmer's appearances in Britain and America are still greeted with fanatical enthusiasm by his vast army of fans.

GARY PLAYER

One of the world's greatest golfers, sharing with Gene Sarazen, Ben Hogan and Jack Nicklaus the feat of winning all four major titles – the U.S. Open (1965), British Open (1959), P.G.A. Championship (1962) and Masters (1961). He also won the British Open in 1968.

His record is an astonishing one.

South African Open Championship seven times, Australian Open Champion six times, winner of the Piccadilly World Match-play Championship four times. Winner of over 75 tournaments, including 13 in the United States where in 17 years he has won over £300,000. He has represented South Africa 10 times in the World Cup.

Throughout his 19 years as a professional he has maintained a high degree of consistency which few others can match, and although he has often spoken of retirement, there seems little likelihood of this at least for another seven or eight years.

A great family man, Player has a farm near Johannesburg where he breeds horses and where he is spending an increasing amount of his time, a sign that he is carrying out the oft-quoted intention of restricting his tournament appearances.

His wife, Vivien, and the five children are among his most fervid supporters with one of the best scrap-books in the business.

LEE TREVINO

The man who brings fun into the game and whether playing good or poor golf invariably seems to hit the headlines.

He really came into the world scene when taking the U.S. Open in 1968 and has been rolling in the cash ever since. On the U.S. tour alone the last four years have produced 10 titles and a little under £250,000 in the bank, while in Britain he was runner-up to Jack Nicklaus in the 1970 Piccadilly Match-play Championship and winner of the British Open Championship in 1971.

With that record he can afford to be funny . . . and the crowd love it.

He did not come on to the tour until he had completed seven years, hard years, as a professional, and if it had not been for his wife, who sent in his first U.S. Open entrance form, Trevino may well have been way out in the wilderness for a few more years. However, that entrance form led him to fifth place in his first Open and on to the road that has brought a much needed air of freshness to many a tournament.

He still lives in El Paso, where he started, with his family of three.

PETER THOMSON

Without question Peter Thomson is the most successful professional of modern times to have ignored the riches of the American tour. He stated categorically several years ago: "The pursuit of the dollar has brought a commercialisation into sport which is frightening. I do not like America or the type of golf they play. I am happy not to play there." Quite a decision for the five-times winner of the British Open Championship, who could undoubtedly have amassed a small fortune by playing a brand of the game he did not enjoy.

His tremendous record in the Open began in 1954 at Royal Birkdale. He kept the title for the next two years, finished runner-up to Bobby Locke in 1957 and regained the crown the following year – four victories and one second place in five years. It was to be seven long years before he again won the coveted title – on the course where it all began, at Birkdale.

Winner of countless titles throughout the world, he is the father-figure of Australian golf, largely responsible for the growth of their lucrative tournament circuit, and leading planner behind a move to establish a world circuit outside America. He is also a successful course architect.

TOMMY AARON (U.S.)

The near-miss champion. A professional since 1960, he was runner-up almost to the point of obsession, before he broke through to take the 1969 Canadian Open. The next year he carried off the Atlantic Classic. Last year seemed no different. No victories, but a third spot three times and a standard of consistency that earned him 30th place in the money list. In 34 tournaments, he was in the money on 29 occasions.
Born February 22, 1937. Height 6 ft. 1 in. Weight 180 lb.

GEORGE ARCHER (U.S.)

Tallest player on the U.S. tour, had first win in the Lucky International, San Francisco. Since has won eight tour events including the 1969 Masters. Finishing fourth in the 1971 money list points to steady performances which included wins in the Andy Williams-San Diego Open and the Greater Hartford Open. He was runner-up in the Monsanto Open, the Sahara International and the Bahamas Open. He was third once, and another three times in the top 10. Winner Los Angeles Open, Greensboro Open, 1972.
Born October 1, 1939. Height 6 ft. 6 in. Weight 200 lb.

162

HARRY BANNERMAN (U.K.)

An inspired three-month period in 1971, when he finished well in the money in 11 tournaments without recording a single win, gained Bannerman a place in the Ryder Cup team which faced America at St. Louis. He was unbeaten in singles encounters in the match, beating Gardner Dickinson and halving with Arnold Palmer. He partnered Bernard Gallacher to a victory over Billy Casper and Miller Barber in the foursomes, but lost at the 18th in partnership with Peter Townsend against Nicklaus and Palmer in the fourball series. Winner of nine Scottish events, including the Scottish P.G.A. in 1967. In that same year he represented Scotland in the World Cup in Mexico with Eric Brown.
Born March 5, 1942. Height 5 ft. 11 in. Weight 12 st. 3 lb.

MILLER BARBER (U.S.)

With less than £4,500 to show for his first four years on the tour, Barber took a back seat to reconsider things. He came back in 1963 and since has been really making news. In the last five years his total winnings have reached almost £170,000. Has six tour wins to his credit and was a member of the U.S. Ryder Cup teams in 1969 and 1971. Last season won the Phoenix Open, was runner-up in the Hawaiian Open, third in the Doral-Eastern, tied third in the Williams-San Diego, tied fourth in the P.G.A. Championship. Winner Dean Martin Open, 1972.
Born March 31, 1931. Height 5 ft. 11 in. Weight 200 lb.

BRIAN BARNES (U.K.)

Consistency the keynote of success. Played in last two Ryder Cup matches. Finished fourth in the 1971 P.G.A. Order of Merit. First P.G.A. victory in 1969, taking the Agfa-color tournament and followed by becoming Coca-Cola Champion. Year later became first British winner of the Wills Masters in Australia. Runner-up Italian Open in 1971. Winner Martini tournament 1972.
Born June 3, 1945. Height 6 ft. 2 in. Weight 15 st. 5 lb.

FRANK BEARD (U.S.)

Since 1963 has won 11 tournaments, been leading money-winner twice, yet few people really know him. Having won the Kentucky Amateur twice before turning professional, he brought to the pro tour an elegant swing and remarkable putting ability in 1962. In 1971, he won the New Orleans, tied second for the Byron Nelson and finished high in the Heritage, Westchester and Tournament of Champions. In 31 events figured in the money lists on 28 occasions to take a final money-winners place of eighth.
Born May 1, 1939. Height 6 ft. Weight 190 lb.

DEANE BEMAN (U.S.)

Following a distinguished amateur career, which included 1960 and 1963 U.S. Amateur Championships, the 1959 British Championship, membership of five U.S. Walker Cup teams, four U.S. World Amateur teams, Beman joined the professional ranks in 1967. And in five years he has won almost £100,000 including three tour victories. In 1971 won the Quad-Cities, was second in the Southern Disney World, tied fourth in Hartford, and finished 22nd in the money-winners list.
Born April 22, 1938. Height 5 ft. 7½ in. Weight 155 lb.

164

MAURICE BEMBRIDGE (U.K.)

A great traveller, playing in over 40 major stroke-play tournaments throughout world last year. Won the Dunlop Masters and finished third in the P.G.A. Order of Merit. Won the Kenya Open (1968) and retained title (1969). Partnered Angel Gallardo to take the Sumrie Clothes Four-ball tournament same year prior to becoming P.G.A. Match-play Champion. Played in the Piccadilly World Match-play Championship 1969.
Born February 21, 1945. Height 5 ft. 7½ in. Weight 11 st. 6 lb.

HOMERO BLANCAS (U.S.)

In 1962, three years before turning professional, Blancas was in the Golf Records Book. That year, when 24, he returned a 55 on the Premier Golf Course in Texas to equal the all-time low-scoring record. In his first year on the tour was awarded the "Rookie-of-the-Year" Award, since when three major wins have come his way. Last year he scored a 63 during the Phoenix Open, but was far from consistent in what was for him a disappointing year. Finished 38th in the money-winners list. Winner Phoenix Open, 1972.
Born March 7, 1938. Height 5 ft. 10 in. Weight 195 lb.

FRED BOOBYER (U.K.)

A reliable performer on the circuit since 1965 when after winning the Ramstein International (Germany) he went on to win the Bowmaker tournament. Two years later represented England in the R.T.V. International tournament in Cork. Turned professional in 1949 and subsequently took the Gloucester and Somerset Championship (1951), West of England Championship (1960), Middlesex Championship (1961). In top 50 of the P.G.A. Order of Merit for fifth time in last six years.
Born January 28, 1928. Height 6 ft. Weight 12 st.

JULIUS BOROS (U.S.)

In 22 years as a professional he has to his credit 18 tour wins including two national titles, the U.S. Open (1952 and 1963) and the P.G.A. Championship (1968). He was Player-of-the-Year twice, in 1952 and 1963, has been four times member of U.S. Ryder Cup teams and top money-winner in 1952 and 1955. And at 47 years of age he was fourth in that same list, dropping but one place for the following year. Last year took part in 24 events, finishing runner-up in the Citrus, tied second in the National Team Championship and third in the Colonial. Took 37th place in the money list.
Born March 3, 1920. Height 6 ft. Weight 200 lb.

HUGH BOYLE (U.K.)

Ryder Cup place in 1967 and represented Ireland in the World Cup same year. Won the Daks tournament in 1966 and year later registered sound victories in the Irish Championship and the Blaxnit tournament. Best achievement recorded in Japan during 1966 when taking the Yomiuri International Open. In 1970 won the Irish Dunlop and the Surrey Open.
Born January 28, 1936. Height 6 ft. Weight 12 st. 11 lb.

GAY BREWER (U.S.)

A well-travelled professional since 1956, he has nine major wins on his card plus the 1965 National Four-ball title. Beaten in a play-off for the Masters in 1966, he made sure the following year with a clear-cut margin. He moved up from 83rd to 44th in the money-winners list last year. In the top 10 of 24 events on seven occasions his figures would have been a lot better but for inconsistencies during final rounds.
Born March 12, 1932. Height 6 ft. Weight 175 lb.

ANDREW BROOKS (U.K.)

Unbeaten in three matches in the 1969 Walker Cup series in Milwaukee, he joined the professional ranks soon after and attained 26th placing in the 1970 P.G.A. Order of Merit in his first year. Represented Scotland at all amateur international levels. First professional success when taking the Cameron Corbet Vase. Last year represented Scotland in the Double Diamond International tournament.

Born December 22, 1946. Height 6 ft. 1 in. Weight 12 st. 7 lb.

ERIC BROWN (U.K.)

Had been unbeaten in four successive Ryder Cup singles before becoming Ryder Cup captain in 1969. Known for his hard-fighting qualities he has instilled much of this enthusiasm into subsequent teams. Winner of 25 events in Britain and Europe. In 1957 took the Dunlop, Masters, Scottish P.G.A., Northern Open and won the Harry Vardon Trophy. Earlier in career which started in 1947, he registered victories in the Swiss, Portuguese and Italian Opens and won the Scottish Professional Championship on eight occasions. Represented Scotland in the World Cup series 12 times. Past captain of the P.G.A.

Born February 15, 1925. Height 5 ft. 10½ in. Weight 12 st. 8 lb.

CHARLES COODY (U.S.)

Winner of 30 titles before turning professional in 1964 he has been a high-ranking money-winner ever since. Although only winning three major titles, including the Masters in 1971, he has been there or thereabouts on numerous occasions. But a little inconsistency has cost him dear. Last year was a typical example. A very poor start to the tour, with but one appearance in the top 10 in 10 events, Coody started a run of six events never out of the top 10, during which time he won the Masters. Finished 16th in the money-winners list.

Born July 13, 1937. Height 6 ft. 2 in. Weight 185 lb.

JOHN COOK (U.K.)

At 16 a member of the England Boys' International team, at 18 Youth team honours and reserve for the senior National team, at 20 English Amateur Champion and a full International. Quite a background before turning professional at 21 in 1970. That year he scored his first major tournament success, winning the Nigerian Open Championship at Lagos. He was runner-up in the same event last season.

Born August 14, 1949. Height 6 ft. Weight 11 st. 8 lb.

169

BRUCE CRAMPTON (Australia)

A sound player, and since 1968, very consistent with several high placings in the money-winners list. One of the top foreign players to compete in the U.S. tour, in that time he has won something near £195,000 with wins in the West End (1968), Hawaiian (1969), Westchester and Western (1970) plus many second and third placings. In 1971 the Western Open win qualified him for the World Series of Golf, he was third in the Cleveland and fourth in the first U.S. Professional Match-play Championship. Second in the 1972 U.S. Open.
Born September 28, 1935. Height 5 ft. 11 in. Weight 180 lb.

GORDON CUNNINGHAM (U.K.)

A professional for 17 years, his early seasons were mainly spent overseas, but in his second year on the P.G.A. tour he took third place in the Penfold tournament. That was in 1968 and he later won the Cutty Sark tournament and the Glasgow Professional Championship. Scottish P.G.A. Champion in 1969, he also won the Uniroyal tournament that year.
Born June 1, 1934. Height 5 ft. 8 in. Weight 11 st.

KIM DABSON (U.K.)

Turned professional in 1969. Met with mixed fortune in early British events. Pipped at the post by Peter Butler in the 1971 Classic International, he had earlier finished fifth in the Martini, and was well placed in the Gallaher Ulster Open and the Benson and Hedges Festival. This earned him 37th place in the P.G.A. Order of Merit, comparing well with his 63rd position of the previous year.
Born July 10, 1952. Height 6 ft. Weight 11 st. 7 lb.

CRAIG DEFOY (U.K.)

One of the few professionals to join the ranks straight from school at the age of 16. It was eight years before he hit world headlines when finishing a sound fourth in the 1971 Open Championship, three strokes behind Lee Trevino. In 1968 he won the Gor-Ray Under-24 tournament, and next year took Lord Derby's Under-23 event followed by success in the Energen Junior Match-play Championship. He began to make impact on major circuits in 1971 when he finished third in the W. D. and H. O. Wills Open, fourth in the Martini, and reached the semi-finals of the Piccadilly Medal. Same year won the "Cock o' the North" in Zambia. Last year won the Mufulira Open, also in Zambia.
Born March 27, 1947. Height 6 ft. 1 in. Weight 11 st. 5 lb.

BRUCE DEVLIN (Australia)

A professional for 11 years and a much travelled golfer, his U.S. tour record shows seven major successes including three, the Bob Hope Classic, Cleveland Open and Alcan, in 1970. That year he finished eleventh in the money-winners list. Best performance in 1971 was to tie runner-up spot in the Tournament of Champions, and finish second in the National Team event. Winner Houston Champions, 1972.
Born October 10, 1937. Height 6 ft. 1 in. Weight 158 lb.

171

GARDNER DICKINSON (U.S.)

Almost gave up the golf tour in 1969 after 16 years of play without a great deal of success, although there had been wins in the Miami Beach, Insurance City Open, Coral Gables Open, Cleveland Open, to mention but four. But in the last two years wins in the Colonial Invitation, and the Atlanta plus a second in the Doral Eastern have proved the wisdom of second thoughts. The Atlanta title came after a sudden death play-off with Jack Nicklaus.
Born September 27, 1927. Height 5 ft. 10 in. Weight 144 lb.

DAVE EICHELBERGER (U.S.)

A brilliant amateur, member of the U.S. Walker Cup team and representative for the U.S. in the Americas Cup, he entered the professional ranks after a short military career. Three years later, in 1970, he began to establish himself. That year saw him move from 132nd on the money-winners list to 88th, and in 1971 he was up in ninth position. During that year he played in 36 major events, was in the money on 31 occasions, took the Milwaukee, finished second in the Williams-San Diego and Greensboro events and was in the top 10 nine times.
Born September 3, 1943. Height 6 ft. 1 in. Weight 185 lb.

LEE ELDER (U.S.)

During the nine years from 1959 to 1967, Elder won 21 of 23 tournaments run by the United Golf Association before joining the pro tour. He has yet to win a tour event, but came near to success last year when finishing tied second for the Thomas Memphis behind Lee Trevino, and tied third for the New Orleans Open. Perhaps his best performance was in 1968 when tied first place with Jack Nicklaus for the American Golf Classic and took him to five holes in the play-off before yielding.
Born July 14, 1934. Height 5 ft. 8 in. Weight 170 lb.

ROGER FIDLER (U.K.)

Appeared in 12 tournaments in Britain and Europe in 1971 to finish a well-merited 33rd in the P.G.A. Order of Merit. Club professional at West Kent since 1960 he has taken the Kent Professional Championship on three occasions. Has same record in the Kent Open Championship. Limited in major tournament play, he has made his own headlines. Last year in the French Open at Biarritz he came in with first round of 63. His best P.G.A. performance has been joint runner-up to Clive Clark in the John Player Trophy at Nottingham in 1970.
Born August 26, 1938. Height 6 ft. 1 in. Weight 12 st. 11 lb.

RAY FLOYD (U.S.)

Hitting headlines with success in the 1960 National Jaycee tournament he turned professional in 1961. Two years later won the St. Petersburg Open and became "Rookie-of-the-Year", and in 1965 he recorded his second success, winning the St. Paul Open. But 1969 was his best year, taking the Jacksonville Open, the American Golf Classic and the P.G.A. Championship to finish eighth in the money-winners list. During 1971 finished second in the Hope Desert Classic and the Massachusetts Classic. He was in the money for 21 events out of 31 to finish 32nd in the list.
Born September 4, 1942. Height 6 ft. Weight 185 lb.

BERNARD GALLACHER (U.K.)

An enthusiastic golfer since early schooldays, at 17 he won the Scottish Stroke-play Championship and represented his country one year later. Turned professional the same year. In 1969 won four tournaments and took the Harry Vardon Trophy as well as representing Britain in the Ryder Cup. He had taken the W. D. and H. O. Wills Open at Moor Park having broken the course record with 63. In Ryder Cup he beat Lee Trevino 4 and 3 and with Maurice Bembridge won 2 and 1 over Trevino and Still. In 1970 he had just one victory and slid to 22nd in the Order of Merit, but he was back in 1971. Following his Scottish P.G.A. success he took the Martini with a fantastic four rounds reading 80–67–68–67. Taking part in his second Ryder Cup, he defeated Coody 2 and 1 in singles and halved with Stockton to keep his unbeaten record.
Born February 9, 1949. Height 5 ft. 9 in. Weight 11 st. 5 lb.

ANGEL GALLARDO (Spain)

Following his first major success in the Portuguese Open in 1967, he has been a popular and successful figure in American, British and European events. In 1969, with Maurice Bembridge as partner, he shared the Sumrie Four-ball tournament. He won the Spanish Open in 1970 and last year was the only European to win on the American continent when taking the Mexican Open. Represented Spain in the World Cup in 1970 and 1971.
Height 5 ft. 7 in. Weight 11 st. 7 lb.

JEAN GARAIALDE (France)

A leading European golfer for the last 11 years, he has been French Champion on nine occasions. Won Open Championships of Spain, France and Germany in 1969. In 1970, apart from again winning the German Open, beat Jack Nicklaus by two strokes to take the Volvo tournament in Sweden.
Born October 2, 1934. Height 5 ft. 10 in. Weight 12 st.

JOHN GARNER (U.K.)

A three-handicap player when 16, he joined the professional ranks that year and has steadily improved. In 1967 was second in the Under-23's Championship, 1969 saw him second in the Algarve Open, second in the Schweppes P.G.A. Championship as well as the Martini International. Ended that year 13th in the P.G.A. Order of Merit. An injury marred his 1970 programme which included second place in the Nigerian Open. Last year he won the Coca-Cola Championship and finished well up in 10 tournaments to earn 12th spot in the P.G.A. Order of Merit and a place in the Ryder Cup team at St. Louis.
Born January 9, 1947. Height 5 ft. 10 in. Weight 10 st. 12 lb.

BOB GOALBY (U.S.)

Won six amateur tournaments in the two years before turning professional in 1957, since when he has been a regular tour player. Most important win was the 1968 Masters, the year Roberto de Vicenzo signed for an incorrect score, but other wins have included Greensboro, Coral Gables, Los Angeles, St. Petersburg, San Diego, Heritage Classic and last year, the Bahamas National. His position in the money-winners list has fluctuated from year to year but is rarely out of the first 60.
Born March 14, 1931. Height 6 ft. Weight 195 lb.

MALCOLM GREGSON (U.K.)

At 16 he reached the final of the French Boys' Championship and represented England and Britain in boys' teams. Turning professional in 1961 he waited three years before his first real success, taking the Gor-Ray Assistants' Championship. Gained worldwide experience during 1965–66, visiting America, the Far East, Australasia and South Africa. In 1967 shared the Indian Open Championship, but lost play-off. Won the Schweppes Championship (his first P.G.A. success), and later took the Daks tournament (retained title in 1968) and shared in the Martini International with Brian Huggett. That year he won the Harry Vardon Trophy. In 1970 he finished 17th in the P.G.A. Order of Merit, but went back to 24th placing last season despite a sound performance in the Open Championship. Winner (with Brian Huggett) of the 1972 Sumrie Four-ball.
Born August 15, 1943. Height 6 ft. Weight 12 st.

DALE HAYES (South Africa)

A scratch player at 15, he proved an outstanding amateur at international level. Twice winner of the South African Stroke-play Championship, he also won the German Amateur Championship, and on first visit to U.S.A. won the World Junior Championship. He also represented his country in the Eisenhower Team Trophy to finish second in individual event. Joined the professional ranks in 1971 and took the Spanish Open Championship that year. Earlier he had won the Newcastle Open in South Africa, and since has taken the Bert Hagerman tournament with a five-stroke margin.
Born July 1, 1952. Height 6 ft. 3½ in. Weight 14 st.

PETER THOMSON, *five times winner of the British Open Championship.*

TOMMY HORTON, *passed over by the selectors for Ryder Cup honours in the last two matches despite his victories in the South African Open and the Long John Match-play Championship.*

HARRY BANNERMAN *(right) gained his Ryder Cup place in 1971 without a major tournament victory to his name, but a golden 11-week period when he finished in the money in every event, assured him of a team place.*

DAI REES *(left)*, *veteran Welsh star and winner*
of major events for 30 years.

MILLER BARBER, *winner of six U.S. tour events.*
Better known as "Mr. X".

JOHN JACOBS *(left) the finest teacher of the game and official coach to many national and international teams. Played in the Ryder Cup of* 1955.

BRUCE CRAMPTON, *the iron man of golf. In his early days on the U.S. tour this tough Australian played for more than 40 weeks without a break.*

JIMMY KINSELLA, *quick-swinging Irish star. Winner of the 1972 Madrid Open.*

JERRY HEARD (U.S.)

A tour player since 1969, his money-winner places have been 129th, 54th, and last year seventh. His change of fortune came midway through 1970 when he followed up high placings in the Cleveland and Philadelphia Opens with a fourth in the Westchester, which pushed him well up the cash list. A win in the American Golf Classic, tied second in the Danny Thomas-Memphis, tied third in the Western, tied fourth in the Crosby National, Citrus and Cleveland events plus high placings in both the National Airlines and Bahamas. Winner Florida Citrus Open and Colonial Invitation, 1972.
Born May 1, 1947. Height 6 ft. Weight 190 lb.

DAVE HILL (U.S.)

Winner of eight tournaments in a professional career which started in 1958 he has been close up on numerous other occasions and has not been lower than 58th in the money-winners list since his first year. In 1969 won three tournaments, the Memphis, Buick and Philadelphia and finished second in the money list with a winning total near the £60,000 mark. One win in 1970 when he retained the Memphis title dropped him eight places, and with limited tournament appearances in 1971 he fell back to 36th place. Best performance was a second in Philadelphia. Winner Monsanto Open, 1972.
Born May 20, 1937. Height 5 ft. 11 in. Weight 155 lb.

LARRY HINSON (U.S.)

An ailing shoulder pulled Hinson back a lot during 1971. In 1969, with a win in the New Orleans, he moved 123 places up the money-winners list to a creditable 36th. And in 1970 without winning a tournament doubled his take to end up in eighth place. Best performance last year was finishing tied for third place in the Robinson Classic, although there were several excellent rounds played including a closing 67 in the American Golf Classic.
Born August 5, 1944. Height 6 ft. 2 in. Weight 158 lb.

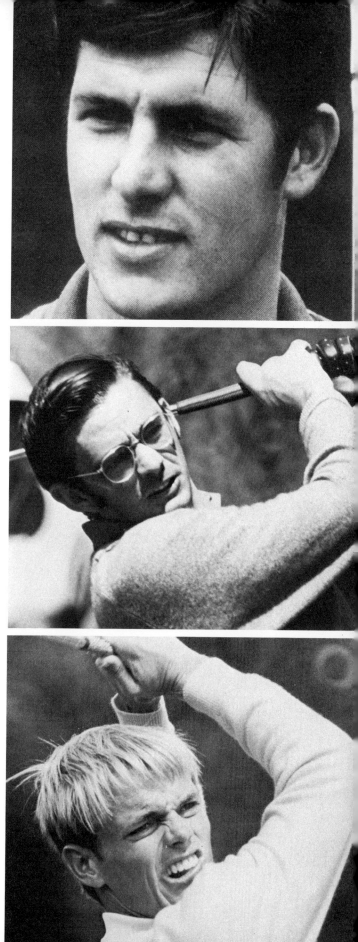

VINCE HOOD (U.K.)

Winner of the Gor-Ray Assistant Professional Championship in 1966, he has maintained a steady P.G.A. rating since. From 33rd placing in the Order of Merit (1967) he moved to 25th in 1968, and last year, following sound performances in the Penfold-Bournemouth and the Dunlop Masters he finished 23rd. Has represented Ireland in the Double Diamond Home International tournament.
Born September 3, 1942. Height 5 ft. 11½ in. Weight 15 st.

TOMMY HORTON (U.K.)

Since taking his first major tournament success in 1968 when winning the R.T.V. International in Cork, Horton has been a regular winner on all major circuits, and rarely outside the top dozen in the P.G.A. Order of Merit. A win in the Tyneside Festival of Golf followed in 1969, but it was in 1970 he really hit the headlines. He became the first British winner of the South African Open Championship, and returning to Britain promptly took the Long John Scotch Whisky Match-play Championship. This second major success of the year came on top of a runner-up spot in both the Piccadilly Medal and Gallaher Ulster Opens. In 1971 he was 13th in the table, but this time won the Gallaher Ulster Open and excelled in the Double Diamond Home International, being unbeaten in five matches. Winner of the 1972 Piccadilly Medal.
Born June 16, 1941. Height 5 ft. 8½ in. Weight 9 st. 11 lb.

DAVID HUISH (U.K.)

A rare name on the touring professional list, yet David Huish finished in the 36th spot of the P.G.A. Order of Merit for 1971 – a year when he put up his best P.G.A. performance to date by finishing runner-up in the Agfa-Gevaert tournament. In Scotland earlier there was a well-merited win in the Uniroyal tournament, and a runners-up place in the Skol. He became Scottish Assistants Champion in 1965, and in the same year took the East of Scotland Stroke-play title.
Born April 23, 1944. Height 6 ft. 2 in. Weight 14 st. 7 lb.

BRIAN HUGGETT (U.K.)

With 16 major tournament successes in 10 years, Huggett is firmly established as a formidable tournament golfer. He has represented Britain on four occasions in Ryder Cup matches, and Wales eight times in the World Cup. A professional since 1951, he has won every major honour in Britain except the Open Championship in which he was runner-up to Peter Thomson in 1965, and third in 1962. In winning the Harry Vardon Trophy for 1968, he had that year registered four big wins, the P.G.A. Match-play Championship, the Sumrie, the Martini International and also the Shell Winter events. In 1970 his major win was the Dunlop Masters, which followed earlier wins in both the Algarve Open and Carrolls International. Finishing eighth in the P.G.A. Order of Merit for 1971, Huggett represented Wales in the Double Diamond International and the World Cup. Winner (with Malcolm Gregson) of the 1972 Sumrie Four-ball.

Born November 18, 1936. Height 5 ft. 6 in. Weight 11 st. 10 lb.

BERNARD HUNT (U.K.)

A successful tournament player for almost 20 years, during which time he has recorded 27 major tournament victories. A professional since 1946, he has played all over the world and has won events in seven overseas countries including the championships of Brazil, Egypt, France, Belgium and Germany. His remarkable success started in 1953 with his first P.G.A. win in the Spalding tournament. Since then there's been a double in the Dunlop Masters, Swallow-Penfold, Penfold, Agfa-Gevaert, Daks, Martini, Carrolls International, Gallaher, Ulster, Piccadilly, and last year the W. D. and H. O. Wills Open. In the top 12 of the Order of Merit list seven times in the past 12 years, he has represented Britain eight times in the Ryder Cup and played six times for England in the World Cup.

Born February 2, 1930. Height 6 ft. 2½ in. Weight 14 st.

GUY HUNT (U.K.)

Steadily climbed the Order of Merit list last year to finish 15th, following a placing of 30th the previous year. Won the Southern P.G.A. Championship 1968 and same year was successful in Lord Derby's Under-23 tournament. Last year reached quarter-finals of the Piccadilly Medal and was runner-up in the Coca-Cola Championship. In the Parmeco tournament a 63 gave him the same placing.
Born January 17, 1947. Height 5 ft. 6 in. Weight 10 st. 8 lb.

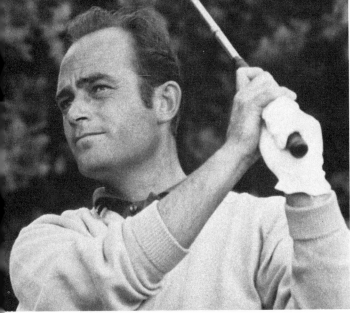

HUGH JACKSON (U.K.)

Taking to the game when 16, he turned professional six years later. In 1968 teamed with Richard Emery to take the Piccadilly Four-ball tournament, and later that year won the Irish Dunlop. In 1970 finished eighth in Open Championship, third in Daks, fourth in Carrolls International. Won the Irish Professional Championship and finished ninth in the Money-winners list. Represented Ireland in the World Cup. Last year he represented Ireland in the Double Diamond Home International and took the Ulster Professional Championship for the sixth time.
Born February 28, 1940. Height 5 ft. 8½ in. Weight 10 st. 9 lb.

DON JANUARY (U.S.)

In 16 tour years he has notched 10 major wins, most important of which was the P.G.A. Championship in 1967. He does not take part in many tournaments during a year, but usually finishes well up the money-winners list, with the high mark in 1963 of ninth placing. That year he won the Tucson and was second in several other events. He was a member of the 1965 Ryder Cup team. Best cheque came from a hole-in-one in the 1961 Palm Springs Classic. It was worth nearly £19,250.
Born November 20, 1929. Height 6 ft. Weight 165 lb.

JIMMY KINSELLA (U.K.)

A sound performer since schooldays (he won three Boys' Championships), he became professional at Castle when 26. Success in Carrolls International early in 1967 was his first big win, but three seasons later he gained 10th position in the P.G.A. Order of Merit, following a series of fine performances in the Alcan International, Long John Scotch Whisky Match-play Championship, and the Penfold. Last year won Irish Dunlop and finished third in Irish Professional Championship. Represented Ireland 1968 and 1969. Winner of 1972 Madrid Open.
Born May 25, 1939. Height 6 ft. Weight 12st. 7 lb.

GEORGE KNUDSON (Canada)

Moves frequently between the U.S. and Canada where he was born and has been a regular tour player for 13 years. Has won almost £140,000 in that time, with 11 major wins on the card. In 1964, apart from the Canadian P.G.A. Championship, he picked up wins at Caracas and Fresno, but his highest placing came a year later when a New Orleans victory helped towards a 22nd position in the money list. Out of touch during 1971, when his highest placing was tied third in the Colonial, Knudson slipped to 60th position which just saved him from qualifying for the 1972 campaign.
Born June 28, 1937. Height 5 ft. 10 in. Weight 165 lb.

BILL LARGE (U.K.)

In 1966 he birdied the last hole to share with Peter Alliss the Martini International. With Jimmy Hitchcock he won the Honda tournament in 1965 and same year was runner-up in the Rediffusion tournament. Third in the Penfold and again third in the Piccadilly Stroke-play tournament in 1967. Up to 12th in the P.G.A. Order of Merit place in 1968, he shared the Alcan International with Christy O'Connor and was runner-up in the W. D. and H. O. Wills Open.
Born July 2, 1937, Height 5 ft. 8 in. Weight 11 st.

GENE LITTLER (U.S.)

A quiet man, Littler has been a popular tour star since 1954, and in the 18 years since has won something like £350,000 with no fewer than 23 tournament successes. He has been in the top 10 of the money-winners list on nine occasions and never lower than 32nd. An amazing record of consistency. Winner of the U.S. Open in 1961, he won the Tournament of Champions three years in a row, 1955–56–57. A member of the Ryder Cup team six times, he won two more titles last year, the Monsanto and the Colonial, but is now the victim of illness.
Born July 21, 1930. Height 5 ft. 9½ in. Weight 165 lb.

LU LIANG HUAN (Formosa)

The man who nearly took the 1971 Open Championship from Lee Trevino, and became a favourite with millions of television viewers. Less than 10 days later he took the French Open with a total of 262. Earlier in 1971 he had won the Thailand Open, and with consistent performances in the Swiss and German Opens he was invited to play in the Piccadilly World Match-play Championship. A leading figure on the Far East circuit, he has some 35 tournament victories to his credit over a period of 18 years.
Height 5 ft. 8 in. Weight 10 st.

DOUG McCLELLAND (U.K.)

Turning professional at 20 after representative honours in Youth Internationals, in 1971 he tied for fourth place in the Daks tournament and later did well in the Swiss Open and also the W. D. and H. O. Wills Open. During the South African tour in 1970–71 he performed well in several important events. He finished in 30th position in the P.G.A. Order of Merit for 1971.

Born November 30, 1949. Height 5 ft. 11½ in. Weight 11 st. 4 lb.

JOHNNY MILLER (U.S.)

As an amateur finished eighth in the 1966 U.S. Open and it was not long before he was drawn towards the professional ranks, making his début in 1969. In two years he has won £55,000 with one major title, the Southern, won last year. He also finished second in the Masters (with Jack Nicklaus) and third in the Jacksonville Open, where he three-putted the last green.

Born April 29, 1947. Height 6 ft. 2 in. Weight 175 lb.

191

BOB MURPHY (U.S.)

Won the Philadelphia and Thunderbird Opens on successive week-ends in 1968 and thoroughly earned the "Rookie-of-the-Year" title – as well as 10th spot in the money-winners list. He dropped back in 1969, but taking the Hartford in 1970 he was back to ninth place with some £45,000 in the bank. Last year was again disappointing, the nearest to success being third in the Crosby National, Houston Champions and the American Golf Classic. He was also tied fourth in the Monsanto Open.

Born February 14, 1943. Height 5 ft. 10 in. Weight 215 lb.

HEDLEY MUSCROFT (U.K.)

A professional since 1954, his first big success came in 1968 with a win in the Evian Open. Same year he finished third in Carrolls International, third in the Alcan International Championship and 11th in the P.G.A. Order of Merit. In 1970 he won the Classic International and finished third (with Lionel Platts) in the Sumrie Better-ball tournament. He has three victories in the Yorkshire Open, three in the Yorkshire Professional Championship and is current holder of the Leeds Open.

Born April 3, 1938. Height 6 ft. 1 in. Weight 15 st.

KEL NAGLE (Australia)

Holder of the 1971 World Seniors' Championship, it was way back in 1954 when Nagle first broke into the news. That year, with Peter Thomson as partner, he won the Canada Cup for Australia, a feat they were to repeat in 1959. In 1960 he won the Centenary British Open at St. Andrews. Has also won the Australian Open, Australian-New Zealand Professional Championship, Canadian Open and French Open. Last year he was also successful in the Volvo tournament in Sweden, runner-up in the Martini, fourth in Carrolls International.
Born December 21, 1920. Height 5 ft. 10½ in. Weight 13 st. 7 lb.

BOBBY NICHOLS (U.S.)

Consistent performer in the big events, and since 1962 has won nine top titles. These include the P.G.A. Championship (1964), Carling World Open (1964), P.G.A. Team (1968), Houston (1962, 1965). He missed the 1967 Masters by one shot and in same year was named for the U.S. Ryder Cup team. Last year did not see a win, but out of 27 events he was placed in the top 10 on seven occasions, headed by a second place in the Western. He returned 34 rounds under 70, and in seven tournaments never had a round over par.
Born April 14, 1936. Height 6 ft. 2 in. Weight 198 lb.

CHRISTY O'CONNOR (U.K.)

A dominating personality in British golf for 16 years and winner of over 20 major tournaments he has won more official money than any other player on the circuit. Has recorded successes in Daks (1959), Irish Hospitals (1960, 1962), Martini (1963 tie and 1964), Senior Service (1965), Alcan International (1968 tie), Dunlop Masters (1956, 1959), P.G.A. Match-play Championship (1957), three wins each in Carrolls International and Gallaher Ulster Open, John Player Classic (1970). Has represented Britain in every Ryder Cup match since 1955, and played 14 times for Ireland in the World Cup.
Born December 21, 1924. Height 5 ft. 10 in. Weight 13 st. 6½ lb.

LIONEL PLATTS (U.K.)

First came into prominence in 1964 with success in the Braemar tournament and a final seventh place in the P.G.A. Order of Merit. The following year he lost a play-off in the Swallow-Penfold, lost to Neil Coles in the final of the P.G.A. Match-play Championship, and lost in a three-way play-off for the Gallaher Ulster Open. A place in the Ryder Cup team was some consolation, and he finished seventh in the P.G.A. list. Last year won the Portuguese Open.

Born October 10, 1934. Height 6 ft. Weight 14 st. 7 lb.

EDDIE POLLAND (U.K.)

At 18, runner-up in the Irish Boys' Championship and one year later he joined the professional ranks. In 1970 won the Irish Assistants' Championship and was runner-up to Peter Oosterhuis in the Coca-Cola Young Professionals' Championship. Three Irish tournaments fell to him in 1971, the Ulster Brick, Ulster Tankard and the Northern Ireland Challenge Cup, but his most notable success was in winning the 36-hole Parmeco Classic at Rushcliffe.

Born June 10, 1947. Height 5 ft. 11 in. Weight 11 st. 7 lb.

DAI REES (U.K.)

Can lay claim to more major tournament successes than any other British golfer at present playing. His first success came in 1936 when winning the *News of the World* Match-play, which he also won in 1938, 1949 and 1950. He has recorded two wins in the Dunlop Masters, and held the Harry Vardon Trophy twice. Has played for Britain nine times in the Ryder Cup, four times as captain (once non-playing captain), and led Britain to victory in 1957. Awarded a C.B.E. for services to golf, his appetite for the game seems insatiable. In 1971, at 58 years of age, he played in 15 P.G.A. tournaments for an average of 73·26 per round. Has represented Wales eight times in World Cup matches, and led his country during the Double Diamond Home International series.
Born March 31, 1913. Height 5 ft. 7 in. Weight 11 st. 7 lb.

DAVID RIDLEY (U.K.)

An up-and-coming young professional. In 1970 finished third in the Gallaher Ulster Open, returning a 66 during the event. In 1971 became Middlesex Professional and Assistants' Champion, while in major events finished seventh in Lord Derby's Under-23 tournament, ninth in the Agfa-Gevaert, and 10th in the Swiss Open. Moved up to 38th place in the P.G.A. Order of Merit.
Born March 26, 1952. Height 5 ft. 9 in. Weight 11 st. 2 lb.

PHIL RODGERS (U.S.)

A professional career of ups and downs started in bright fashion in 1961 and 1962 when two major wins, the Tucson and the Los Angeles, boosted a 24-year-old newcomer to 11th money-winners place. And in 1963 came the Texas and a second to Bob Charles in the British Open. Then came the slump. A quiet two years before another double in 1966 with the Buick and Doral and back to sixth place. From 1967 to 1970 Rodgers was way down into the 60-plus range, but 1971 saw the second revival. No wins but in the money 30 times in 35 starts.
Born April 3, 1938. Height 5 ft. 8 in. Weight 170 lb.

BOB ROSBURG (U.S.)

A strange record over 19 years. In 1959 winner of the P.G.A. Championship, and second in the U.S. Open gave him headlines and a best-ever seventh placing in the money-winners list. He had been moving up there for the seven previous years with several sound performances such as wins in the Brawley Open, Miami, Motor City and San Diego. Since then successes have been few and far between, the sole exception being the Crosby National in 1961. Last year Rosburg earned more money than ever before with third place in the U.S. Open, a fifth in the Canadian Open and a course record of 64 in the Houston Champions. Winner Bob Hope Classic, 1972.

Born October 21, 1926. Height 5 ft. 11 in. Weight 185 lb.

MASON RUDOLPH (U.S.)

In the top 30 all-time earners with nearly £145,000 in 12 years on the tour. Yet he has only six tour victories to his name, the Golden Gates, Haig and Haig Mixed Foursome, Fig Garden Village, New Orleans, Thunderbird and Green Island. As an amateur he was a member of the U.S. Walker Cup and Americas teams in 1956, the 1950 U.S. Junior Champion and semi-finalist in the 1957 Amateur.

Born May 23, 1934. Height 5 ft. 11 in. Weight 185 lb.

RONNIE SHADE (U.K.)

A professional since 1968, he won the Ben Sayers tournament in 1969, followed by success in Carrolls International. That year saw him 20th in the P.G.A. Order of Merit. Took the Scottish P.G.A. Championship in 1970, was runner-up in the Long John Scotch Whisky Match-play Championship, just failed to retain the Carrolls title, but moved up to 14th final placing. As an amateur had won the Scottish Amateur five times in succession, the English Open Stroke-play Championship three times, and represented the British team in Walker Cup four times.
Born October 15, 1938. Height 5 ft. 11 in. Weight 11 st. 3 lb.

TOM SHAW (U.S.)

Two years stand out in his short, but somewhat odd, professional career. In 1969 he won the Doral and Avco Opens and promptly jumped from 100th to 16th place in the money-winners list. And this after being seriously injured in a car crash the year before, when it was suggested he would be unlikely to play golf again. A quiet 1970 came next, but last year he was really back in the picture with a clear-cut win in the Bing Crosby, followed by another outstanding below par win in the Hawaiian Open. Despite failing to make money in 13 of 32 starts, he ended in 15th place with £37,000.
Born December 13, 1942. Height 5 ft. 10 in. Weight 180 lb.

DAN SIKES (U.S.)

Joining the tour when 29 he has won six events, the peak money-winning list period being in 1967 (5th) and 1968 (8th). During those two years, the Jacksonville, Philadelphia, Florida Citrus and Minnesota titles came his way. The years 1970 and 1971 were not so productive, but second place in the Phoenix last year restored a little confidence. During his Army career he won the All-Army Championship and just before becoming a professional he won the U.S. Public Links Championship.
Born December 7, 1930. Height 6 ft. 1 in. Weight 185 lb.

PADDY SKERRITT (U.K.)

Convincing win in the Southern Ireland Professional Championship in 1966. He was a member of Ireland's team in the R.T.V. Internationals and played well in the Carrolls International, but it was 1970, with a popular win in the Alcan International Championship at Portmarnock and success in the Irish Match-play Championship that consolidated his position. In 1971 he represented Ireland in the Double Diamond Home Internationals and was runner-up in the Irish Dunlop.
Born May 30, 1930. Height 5 ft. 8 in. Weight 12 st. 7 lb.

J. C. SNEAD (U.S.)

Starting his professional life in 1964, it was four years later before a venture was made on to the tour. It was a slow start, his first three money-winners list returns reading: 280, 121 and 122. But 1971 saw a startling change. Within the space of three weeks two big titles were in the bag. First came the Tucson with a final round of 66, and two weeks later 66 and 69 final rounds brought in the Doral title. He had four more top 10 finishes, including a second in the Hartford. A member of the 1971 U.S. Ryder Cup team he was unbeaten in his four matches. Winner Philadelphia Classic, 1972.
Born October 14, 1941. Height 6 ft. 2 in. Weight 205 lb.

RAMON SOTA (Spain)

Three Open Championships in 1971, the Algarve Open, Italian, and later a win in the Dutch Open, put him firmly in the No. 1 spot in Europe. Having won the Portuguese Open towards the end of 1970, Sota was at the beginning of a successful streak which also included second in the Italian B.P. Open, third in the Spanish Open, fourth in the Madrid Open. Highest placing in Britain was fifth in the Agfa-Gevaert, but consistency in 11 P.G.A. tournaments earned him a 10th placing in the Order of Merit. A leading player for 12 years, he has been four times Spanish Professional Champion, winner of the French Open as well as the Championships of Puerto Rico and Madrid.
Born April 23, 1938. Height 5 ft. 7 in. Weight 12 st. 10 lb.

DAVE STOCKTON (U.S.)

A remarkably consistent performer, one who rarely makes news, but is always very high up in the lists. In just eight years as a professional he has won £160,000 and six tournaments. These include the P.G.A. Championship in 1971, the Cleveland, Milwaukee, and last year the Massachusetts. Last year saw a somewhat shortened programme of events, but in 27 starts Stockton was in the money 24 times, in the top 10 six times, to finish 19th in the money-winners list.
Born November 2, 1941. Height 5 ft. 11½ in. Weight 180 lb.

DAVID TALBOT (U.K.)

Came into the professional ranks in 1952 and it was 11 years later, following many regional successes, that he began to be noticed. That year, 1963, he finished third in the Swallow-Penfold tournament, since when he has rarely been outside the top 30 in the P.G.A. Order of Merit. Won the Schweppes P.G.A. Championship in 1968. Last year played well in the Spanish Open (sixth) before finishing third in the Parmeco Invitation.
Born November 16, 1936. Height 6 ft. Weight 12 st. 8½ lb.

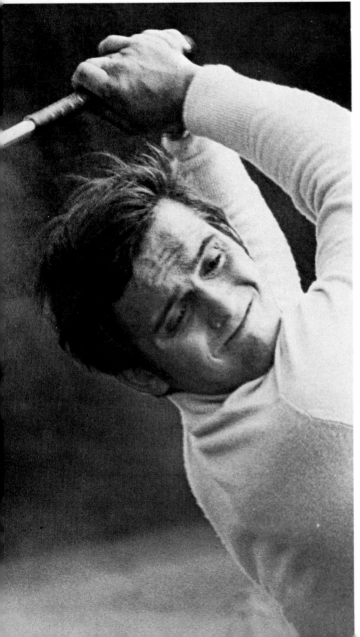

PETER TOWNSEND (U.K.)

Has won seven major titles and represented Britain in the 1969 and 1971 Ryder Cup matches. As an amateur Townsend won the British Boys' and Youths' titles, played in the Walker Cup team which tied with America in Baltimore and added the English Stroke-play crown before turning professional. His only win in 1967 was the Dutch Open, but he followed with a brilliant year in 1968, winning the Piccadilly P.G.A. Championship and the Coca-Cola in Britain and the Western Australian Open. He was also second to defending champion Gay Brewer in the Alcan Golfer of the Year Championship at Royal Birkdale. Having gained his American player's card he spent most of 1969–70 on the U.S. circuit without a win. Returning to Europe in 1971 he won the Swiss Open and the Walworth-Aloyco in Italy, and finished third in the Spanish Open, third in the Daks and fifth in the Dunlop Masters.
Born September 16, 1946. Height 5 ft 8½ in. Weight 11 st. 3 lb.

PETER TUPLING (U.K.)

A British Boy Champion, member of Walker Cup team, Yorkshire Amateur Champion and leading amateur in the Open Championship for 1969. Joined professional ranks early in 1970. He made an immediate impact with a tie for fourth place in the Daks tournament. In 1971 he shared second place in the W. D. and H. O. Wills Open, with final round of 69. *Born April 6, 1950. Height 6 ft. 2 in. Weight 13 st. 1 lb.*

DAVID VAUGHAN (U.K.)

First representative honours in 1971 for Wales in the Double Diamond Home International tournament. This followed a year of consistency with success in Lord Derby's Under-23 Championship and the Liverpool and District Open Championship, a fourth in the Welsh Open, sixth in the Daks and high placings in the Dunlop Masters and the Classic International. He finished 26th in the P.G.A. Order of Merit. *Born June 26, 1948. Height 5 ft. 8 in. Weight 10 st. 10 lb.*

ROBERTO de VICENZO (Argentina)

A professional since 1940 and something like 130 tournament wins on the record card. And that includes 30 national Opens! Represented Argentina 13 times in World Cup events, has been Champion of that country on seven occasions, won the British Open in 1967, a career highlight, almost won the U.S. Masters in 1968 when he missed a play-off by signing a wrong score-card, and in 1971 recorded a 69·89 stroke average in eight British and European tournaments. *Born April 14, 1923. Height 6 ft. 2 in. Weight 12 st. 11 lb.*

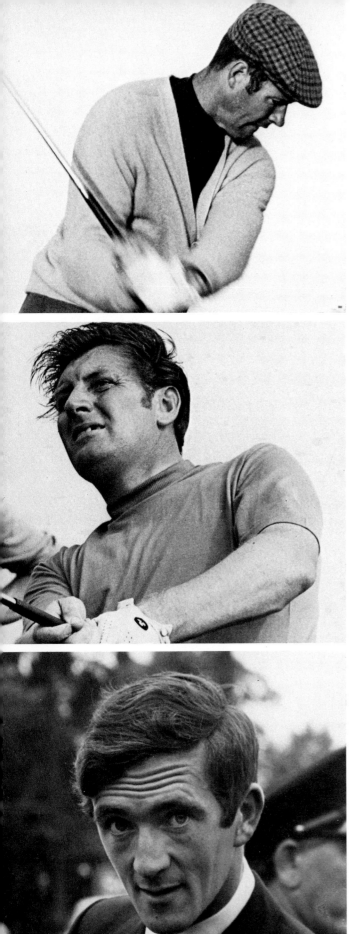

TOM WEISKOPF (U.S.)

A big hitter, within three years of becoming a professional he was well to the fore in tour matters. Success in the Williams-San Diego and Buick in 1968 showed the possibilities as he moved to third in the money-winners list. An Army call-up stopped activities until 1969, but despite no more titles, he was no further back than 18th, and with another £40,000 added dropped but one place in 1970. Last year he was back to his best form with a powerful performance in the Kemper Open to beat Lee Trevino, Gary Player and Dale Douglass in a play-off. Later he took the Philadelphia Classic, tied for fourth place in the Bing Crosby, again in the Florida Citrus, tied for fifth in the U.S. Professional Match-play Championship. He finally finished 12th, with a scoring average of 71·3 over 32 events. Winner Jackie Gleason Classic, 1972.
Born November 9, 1942. Height 6 ft. 3 in. Weight 190 lb.

GEORGE WILL (U.K.)

Biggest win, in a professional career that started in 1957, came in 1965, when with 24 points he won the Esso Golden Round Robin tournament. Consistency has been the key-note of his play, having finished high in the P.G.A. Order of Merit every year since 1964, but tournament appearances now limited. As an amateur he won the Scottish Boys' Championship, also the British Youths' Championship.
Born April 16, 1937. Height 6 ft. Weight 14 st.

PETER WILCOCK (U.K.)

Winner of the Northern Young Professionals Championship in 1968 and 1969. Runner-up in the 1970 Daks tournament. That same year he was seventh in the Martini International and 10th in the Gallaher Ulster Open, and ended 24th in the P.G.A. Order of Merit list. Last year he qualified for the last round of several major tournaments, finishing 16th in the Classic International and 17th in the German Open. In 1972 he won the Italian B.P. Open.
Born November 18, 1945. Height 5 ft. 11 in. Weight 11 st.

GUY WOLSTENHOLME (Australia)

Turned professional in 1960 following several years as an amateur of international standing. He was English Amateur Champion in 1956 and 1959, twice represented Britain in Walker Cup matches and the Eisenhower Trophy. Took the German Amateur twice and won the Brabazon Trophy. In 1961 won the Southern P.G.A., since when major tournament successes have followed at regular intervals. The Jeyes tournament in 1963, Schweppes P.G.A. Champion in 1966, Kenya and Danish Opens 1967, Dutch Open Champion 1969, Endeavour Masters (Australia) and Victor Harbour in 1970. Now resident in Australia, he represented his new country against Japan in a 1971 international in a year which brought him four more titles. These were the Kuzahar Open, City of Aukland Open, South Australian Open and Victorian Open.
Born March 8, 1931. Height 6 ft. 4 in. Weight 13 st. 7 lb.

BERT YANCY (U.S.)

Averaging something like £20,000 a year for every one of his eight years on the tour. Yet in that time only six titles have come his way being the Azalea, Memphis, Portland in 1966, Dallas in 1967, Atlanta in 1969, Crosby National in 1970. In 1971 he was second on two occasions, in the Colonial and the Robinson, third in the Hope Desert Classic and third-tied in the Bahamas National. He was in the money 28 times in 33 tournaments and ended 20th in the money-winners list.
Born August 6, 1938. Height 6 ft. 1 in. Weight 185 lb.

The British Order of Merit 1971

		POINTS	TNMTS	STROKES	ROUNDS	AVERAGE	PRIZE-MONEY
1	P. Oosterhuis	1292·5	17	4019	57	70·50	£9,269·50
2	N. Coles	1285·5	18	—	—	—	10,479·77
3	M. Bembridge	1222·5	18	4224	59	71·59	3,643·32
4	B. Barnes	1215·5	19	4893	68	71·95	2,251·28
5	P. Townsend	1215·0	20	—	—	—	2,669·76
6	H. Bannerman	1206·0	18	4395	61	72·05	3,217·04
7	P. Butler	1202·0	21	4818	67	71·91	6,060·22
8	B. Huggett	1196·0	19	4026	56	71·89	4,049·15
9	B. Gallacher	1179·5	18	3968	55	72·14	3,002·58
10	H. Boyle	1154·5	20	4564	63	72·44	1,871·20
11	R. Sota	1154·5	11	2917	41	71·14	2,262·99
12	J. Garner	1151·0	21	4755	66	72·04	3,506·00
13	T. Horton	1141·0	19	4091	56	73·05	3,135·05
14	B. Hunt	1122·5	16	—	—	—	3,863·90
15	G. Hunt	1110·0	18	4298	59	72·84	1,513·27
16	H. Jackson	1104·5	19	4232	58	72·96	1,482·93
17	S. Brown	1061·5	16	3858	53	72·79	2,511·85
18	L. Platts	1055·5	17	—	—	—	995·86
19	C. Clark	1034·0	19	4323	59	73·27	521·48
20	D. Talbot	1015·5	16	3969	54	73·50	563·75
21	J. Kinsella	1010·5	15	3212	44	73·00	1,619·06
22	D. Hayes	1003·5	12	2886	40	72·15	1,864·43
23	V. Hood	1002·5	13	—	—	—	1,200·11
24	M. Gregson	997·5	18	3732	51	73·17	655·62
25	H. Muscroft	988·5	16	3583	49	73·12	716·19
26	D. Vaughan	986·5	18	3562	49	72·69	1,152·32
27	P. Skerritt	976·5	16	3299	45	73·31	1,047·22
28	E. Brown	975·5	18	3691	50	73·82	1,888·69
29	R. Shade	973·5	17	3609	49	73·65	1,275·11
30	D. McClelland	971·0	19	4005	54	74·16	655·54
31	F. Boobyer	970·0	16	3243	44	73·70	483·78
32	C. DeFoy	969·0	17	3330	45	74·00	3,343·69
33	R. Fidler	945·0	12	2688	37	72·64	432·03
34	W. Large	928·0	18	3829	52	73·63	698·19
35	P. Wilcock	923·0	17	3406	46	74·04	379·44
36	D. Huish	914·0	13	2650	36	73·61	963·60
37	K. Dabson	907·0	15	2533	35	72·37	1,756·60
38	D. Ridley	898·5	17	3544	48	73·83	809·16
39	D. Small	898·5	15	3338	45	74·17	339·37
40	C. O'Connor, Snr.	895·0	10	2097	29	72·31	1,627·40
41	B. Wolstenholme	893·0	14	—	—	—	649·19
42	R. de Vicenzo	869·0	8	2027	29	69·89	1,742·31
43	P. Thomson	864·5	9	2176	31	70·19	3,856·38
44	P. Leonard	864·0	16	3134	42	74·61	319·92
45	W. Cunningham	861·5	14	2888	39	74·05	954·28
46	G. Will	850·5	15	2894	39	74·20	345·63
47	A. Brooks	833·5	16	2835	38	74·60	467·05
48	N. Wood	828·0	15	2965	40	74·12	350·94
49	D. Rees	824·0	15	2784	38	73·26	1,009·74
50	E. Polland	820·0	14	—	—	—	341·73
51	R. Vines	799·5	11	2409	33	73·00	335·12
52	J. Newton	799·0	12	2882	39	73·89	244·35
53	W. Godfrey	782·0	8	2172	30	72·40	392·78
54	K. Ashdown	774·5	14	2827	38	74·39	409·81
55	D. Jagger	745·5	14	2687	36	74·63	329·82
56	D. Webster	745·0	11	2083	28	74·39	387·39
57	L. Tupling	738·5	13	2731	37	73·81	1,359·90
58	D. Butler	736·0	12	2237	30	74·56	153·80
59	P. Cowen	732·5	14	2830	38	74·47	385·40

60	J. Cook	718·0	16	2235	30	74·50	112·63
61	D. Scanlan	707·0	10	1843	25	73·72	369·27
62	L. Lu	697·0	8	1774	25	70·96	5,777·92
63	D. Llewellyn	690·0	13	2530	34	74·41	435·50
64	J. Hudson	675·5	10	1472	20	73·60	473·96
65	P. Harvey	639·0	11	2155	29	74·31	108·03
66	N. Hunt	631·5	12	2271	31	73·25	459·53
67	C. O'Connor, Jnr.	610·5	12	—	—	—	112·37
68	A. Grubb	605·5	10	2219	30	73·96	707·12
69	T. Britz	605·0	6	1574	22	71·54	305·76
70	J. Martin	598·0	9	1932	26	74·30	311·78
71	G. Marsh	593·5	6	1433	20	71·65	175·40
72	A. Palmer	588·0	11	—	—	—	196·89
73	A. Gallardo	587·5	6	1578	22	71·72	22·00
74	D. Swaelens	579·5	7	1762	24	73·41	129·28
75	C. Baker	569·0	12	2479	33	75·12	362·93
76	J. Gallardo	568·5	6	1420	20	71·00	—
77	F. Molina	559·0	7	1590	22	72·27	245·37
78	M. Murphy	555·0	12	1499	20	74·95	180·37
79	V. Barrios	550·5	7	1753	24	73·04	204·28
80	P. McGuirk	550·0	14	2120	28	75·71	338·56
81	M. Ingham	549·5	10	2036	27	75·40	136·49
82	C. Greene	547·5	8	1699	23	73·86	221·49
83	D. Jones	544·0	—	—	—	—	246·11
84	E. Della Torre	540·0	5	1425	20	71·25	—
85	T. Lopez	514·0	6	1455	20	72·75	72·50
86	A. Jacklin	510·0	6	1189	17	69·94	8,502·81
87	D. Sewell	505·0	5	1014	14	72·42	1,046·87
88	K. Bousfield	489·5	9	1599	22	72·68	306·03
89	J. Panton	488·5	8	1603	22	72·86	585·75
90	W. Murray	486·0	9	1479	20	73·95	143·50
91	J. Fowler	481·5	12	—	—	—	280·22
92	V. Baker	476·0	8	1457	20	72·85	74·37
93	P. Toussaint	474·0	11	1943	26	74·73	218·65
94	V. Fernandez	471·5	4	1122	16	70·12	297·28
95	K. Nagle	469·5	6	1557	22	70·77	3,273·88
96	E. Whitehead	469·5	10	1713	23	74·47	266·42
97	J. O'Leary	468·5	8	2027	27	75·14	456·33
98	L. Hooker	457·5	12	1721	23	74·82	122·67
99	R. Emery	455·0	7	1032	14	73·71	174·03
100	F. Abreu	451·5	6	1547	21	73·66	60·00

1	Jack Nicklaus	$244,490.50		51	Kermit Zarley	49,105.80
2	Lee Trevino	231,202.97		52	Larry Hinson	48,604.50
3	Arnold Palmer	209,603.77		53	Mike Hill	48,188.00
4	George Archer	147,769.10		54	John Schlee	47,815.94
5	Gary Player	120,916.79		55	Labron Harris, Jnr.	46,922.51
6	Miller Barber	117,359.25		56	Bob E. Smith	44,595.54
7	Jerry Heard	112,389.02		57	Ken Still	43,660.42
8	Frank Beard	112,337.80		58	Pete Brown	43,599.73
9	Dave Eichelberger	108,312.36		59	Jim Colbert	42,743.16
10	Billy Casper	107,276.07		60	George Knudson	41,634.86
11	Bruce Crampton	106,736.26		61	Dick Lotz	41,517.14
12	Tom Weiskopf	106,538.33		62	Mason Rudolph	41,292.82
13	Hale Irwin	99,473.40		63	Jim Jamieson	40,804.25
14	Gene Littler	98,687.69		64	Jim Weichers	40,110.74
15	Tom Shaw	96,220.83		65	George Johnson	39,893.81
16	Charles Coody	94,947.29		66	Bert Greene	38,296.63
17	J. C. Snead	92,929.90		67	Ralph Johnston	37,947.33
18	Johnny Miller	91,081.54		68	Terry Dill	37,541.15
19	Dave Stockton	85,738.02		69	Larry Ziegler	36,751.82
20	Bert Yancey	84,205.37		70	Lionel Hebert	32,221.18
21	Bob Lunn	83,892.83		71	R. H. Sikes	31,608.70
22	Deane Beman	82,747.72		72	Grier Jones	30,929.83
23	Lou Graham	82,575.10		73	Herb Hooper	30,702.38
24	DeWitt Weaver	76,256.62		74	Juan Rodriguez	30,390.45
25	Dale Douglass	76,070.09		75	Roy Pace	30,166.50
26	Bobby Mitchell	75,891.23		76	John Lotz	29,701.95
27	Bob Murphy	75,301.84		77	Howie Johnson	28,856.25
28	Bobby Nichols	74,205.36		78	Bob Dickson	28,122.05
29	Hubert Green	73,439.63		79	Bob Stone	28,055.45
30	Tommy Aaron	71,573.25		80	Larry Wood	27,049.70
31	Phil Rodgers	71,399.59		81	Chuck Courtney	27,030.83
32	Ray Floyd	70,607.02		82	Ted Hayes	25,707.18
33	Don January	66,388.02		83	Orville Moody	25,256.74
34	Rod Funseth	63,567.41		84	John Schroeder	25,181.51
35	Gibby Gilbert	62,501.31		85	Doug Sanders	24,891.21
36	Dave Hill	61,410.40		86	Ron Cerrudo	24,723.67
37	Julius Boros	60,524.74		87	Hugh Royer	24,402.23
38	Homero Blancas	58,796.43		88	Wilf Homenuik	24,206.04
39	Fred Marti	58,740.27		89	Randy Wolff	23,951.57
40	Gardner Dickinson	58,542.36		90	Charles Sifford	23,916.74
41	Bob Charles	58,016.76		91	Paul Harney	23,661.31
42	Bob Rosburg	56,044.54		92	Mac McLendon	23,376.98
43	Bud Allin	55,786.49		93	Don Bies	22,771.92
44	Gay Brewer	55,444.88		94	Sam Snead	22,258.92
45	Art Wall	54,644.20		95	Johnny Pott	22,249.16
46	Jerry McGee	54,359.67		96	Hal Underwood	22,082.95
47	Dan Sikes	52,202.41		97	Dick Crawford	21,896.03
48	Bruce Devlin	51,175.11		98	Babe Hiskey	21,566.47
49	Lee Elder	49,933.86		99	Al Gieberger	20,848.72
50	Bob Goalby	49,203.78		100	Steve Reid	20,195.29

Britain Tournament Winners 1971

DATE	PURSE	TOURNAMENT	WINNER	PRIZE-MONEY
May 6–8	£8,000	Penfold	**Neil Coles**	£1,463
May 20–22	5,000	Agfa-Gevaert	**Peter Oosterhuis**	975
June 3–5	5,000	Daks	**Brian Huggett**	804
June 10–12	7,000	Martini	**Bernard Gallacher**	1,250
June 17–20	10,000	Carrolls	**Neil Coles**	1,950
June 24–26	6,000	Gallaher Ulster	**Tommy Horton**	1,316
June 28–29	3,000	Sunbeam Electric	**Peter Oosterhuis**	585
July 7–10	6,000	Open Championship	**Lee Trevino**	5,500
Aug 4–7	6,000	Classic International	**Peter Butler**	975
Aug 11–14	10,000	Piccadilly Medal	**Peter Oosterhuis**	1,463
Aug 18–21	12,000	Benson and Hedges	**Tony Jacklin**	1,950
Sept 22–25	10,000	Wills Open	**Bernard Hunt**	1,950
Sept 29–Oct 2	10,000	Dunlop Masters	**Maurice Bembridge**	1,706
Oct 7–9	25,000	Piccadilly World Match-play Championship	**Gary Player**	8,500

Tony Jacklin

Bernard Hunt

Maurice Bembridge

Gary Player

American Tournament Winners 1971

DATE	PURSE	TOURNAMENT	WINNER	PRIZE-MONEY	MARGIN	SCORE
Jan 7–10	$110,000	Campbell-Los Angeles	**Bob Lunn**	$22,000	Play-off	274
		Lunn defeated Casper on 4th hole, birdie				
Jan 14–17	135,000	Crosby National	**Tom Shaw**	27,000	2	278
Jan 21–24	125,000	Phoenix	**Miller Barber**	25,000	2	261
Jan 28–31	150,000	Williams-Dan Diego	**George Archer**	30,000	3	272
Feb 4–7	200,000	Hawaiian	**Tom Shaw**	40,000	1	273
Feb 10–14	140,000	Hope Desert Classic	**Arnold Palmer**	28,000	Play-off	342
		Palmer defeated Floyd on 1st hole, birdie				
Feb 18–21	110,000	Tucson	***J. C. Snead**	22,000	1	273
Feb 25–28	200,000	P.G.A. Championship	**Jack Nicklaus**	40,000	2	281
Mar 4–7	150,000	Doral-Eastern	**J. C. Snead**	30,000	1	275
Mar 11–14	150,000	Florida Citrus	**Arnold Palmer**	30,000	1	270
Mar 18–21	125,000	Jacksonville	**Gary Player**	25,000	Play-off	281
		Player defeated Underwood on 2nd hole, par				
Mar 25–28	200,000	National Airlines	**Gary Player**	40,000	2	274
April 1–4	190,000	Greensboro	***Brian Allin**	38,000	Play-off	275
		Allin defeated Funseth and Eichelberger on 1st hole, birdie				
April 8–11	198,000	Masters	**Charles Coody**	25,000	2	279
April 15–18	150,000	Monsanto	**Gene Littler**	30,000	3	276
April 22–25	165,000	Tournament of Champions	**Jack Nicklaus**	33,000	8	279
April 22–25	60,000	Tallahassee	**Lee Trevino**	12,000		273
April 29– May 2	125,000	New Orleans	**Frank Beard**	25,000	1	276
May 6–9	125,000	Byron Nelson	**Jack Nicklaus**	25,000	2	274
May 13–16	125,000	Houston/Champions	***Hubert Green**	25,000	Play-off	280
		Green defeated January on 1st hole, birdie				
May 20–23	125,000	Colonial National	**Gene Littler**	25,000	1	283
May 27–30	175,000	Danny Thomas Memphis	**Lee Trevino**	35,000	4	268
June 3–6	125,000	Atlanta	**Gardner Dickinson**	25,000	Play-off	275
		Dickinson defeated Nicklaus on 1st hole, par				
June 10–13	150,000	Kemper	**Tom Weiskopf**	30,000	Play-off	277
		Weiskopf defeated Trevino, Douglass, Player on 1st hole, birdie				
June 16–20	200,000	U.S. Open	**Lee Trevino**	30,000	Play-off	280
		Trevino defeated Nicklaus, 68–71, 18 holes				
June 24–27	150,000	Cleveland	***Bobby Mitchell**	30,000	7	262
July 1–4	150,000	Canadian Open	**Lee Trevino**	30,000	Play-off	275
		Trevino defeated Wall on 1st hole, birdie				
July 8–11	125,000	Milwaukee	***Dave Eichelberger**	25,000	1	270
July 15–18	150,000	Western	**Bruce Crampton**	30,000	2	279
July 22–25	250,000	Westchester	**Arnold Palmer**	50,000	5	270
July 29– Aug 1	200,000	National Team Chp.	**Arnold Palmer & Jack Nicklaus**	20,000 each	6	257
Aug 5–8	150,000	American Golf Classic	***Jerry Heard**	30,000	3	275
Aug 12–15	165,000	Massachusetts	**Dave Stockton**	33,000	1	275
Aug 19–22	150,000	Philadelphia	**Tom Weiskopf**	30,000	1	274
Aug 25–29	200,000	U.S. Prof. Match-play Chp.	***DeWitt Weaver**	35,000	6	
		Weaver defeated Phil Rodgers in final, 71–77				
Sept 3–6	110,000	Hartford	**George Archer**	22,000	Play-off	268
		Archer defeated J. C. Snead, Lou Graham on 1st hole, birdie				
Sept 9–12	100,000	Southern	***Johnny Miller**	20,000	5	267
Sept 23–26	100,000	Robinson	***Labron Harris, Jnr.**	20,000	Play-off	274
		Harris defeated Yancey on 3rd hole, birdie				
Oct 21–24	150,000	Kaiser	**Billy Casper**	30,000	4	269
Oct 28–31	135,000	Sahara	**Lee Trevino**	27,000	1	280
Nov 25–28	110,000	Heritage	***Hale Irwin**	22,000	1	279
Dec 2–5	150,000	Disney World	**Jack Nicklaus**	30,000	3	273
Dec 9–12	130,000	Bahamas National	**Bob Goalby**	26,000	1	275

* First-time winner on Tour

Open Championship

THE BELT

YEAR	WINNER	VENUE	SCORE
1860	**W. Park, Musselburgh**	Prestwick	174
1861	**Tom Morris, Snr., Prestwick**	Prestwick	163
1862	**Tom Morris, Snr., Prestwick**	Prestwick	163
1863	**W. Park, Musselburgh**	Prestwick	168
1864	**Tom Morris, Snr., Prestwick**	Prestwick	167
1865	**A. Strath, St. Andrews**	Prestwick	162
1866	**W. Park, Musselburgh**	Prestwick	169
1867	**Tom Morris, Snr., St. Andrews**	Prestwick	170
1868	**Tom Morris, Jnr., St. Andrews**	Prestwick	157
1869	**Tom Morris, Jnr., St. Andrews**	Prestwick	154
1870	**Tom Morris, Jnr., St. Andrews**	Prestwick	149

THE CUP

YEAR	WINNER	VENUE	SCORE
1872	**Tom Morris, Jnr., St. Andrews**	Prestwick	166
1873	**Tom Kidd, St. Andrews**	St. Andrews	179
1874	**Mungo Park, Musselburgh**	Musselburgh	159
1875	**Willie Park, Musselburgh**	Prestwick	166
1876	**Bob Martin, St. Andrews**	St. Andrews	176

(David Strath tied but refused to play off)

YEAR	WINNER	VENUE	SCORE
1877	**Jamie Anderson, St. Andrews**	Musselburgh	160
1878	**Jamie Anderson, St. Andrews**	Prestwick	157
1879	**Jamie Anderson, St. Andrews**	St. Andrews	170
1880	**Bob Ferguson, Musselburgh**	Musselburgh	162
1881	**Bob Ferguson, Musselburgh**	Prestwick	170
1882	**Bob Ferguson, Musselburgh**	St. Andrews	171
1883	**W. Fernie, Dumfries**	Musselburgh	159

After a tie with Bob Ferguson, Musselburgh

YEAR	WINNER	VENUE	SCORE
1884	**Jack Simpson, Carnoustie**	Prestwick	160
1885	**Bob Martin, St. Andrews**	St. Andrews	171
1886	**D. Brown, Musselburgh**	Musselburgh	157
1887	**W. Park, Jnr., Musselburgh**	Prestwick	161
1888	**Jack Burns, Warwick**	St. Andrews	171
1889	**W. Park, Jnr., Musselburgh**	Musselburgh	155

After a tie with Andrew Kirkaldy

YEAR	WINNER	VENUE	SCORE
1890	**Mr. John Ball, Royal Liverpool**	Prestwick	164
1891	**Hugh Kirkaldy, St. Andrews**	St. Andrews	166

After 1891 the competition was extended to 72 holes and for the first time entry money was imposed

YEAR	WINNER	VENUE	SCORE
1892	**Mr. H. H. Hilton, Royal Liverpool**	Muirfield	305
1893	**W. Auchterlonie, St. Andrews**	Prestwick	322
1894	**J. H. Taylor, Winchester**	Sandwich	326
1895	**J. H. Taylor, Winchester**	St. Andrews	322
1896	**H. Vardon, Ganton**	Muirfield	316

After a tie with J. H. Taylor. Replay scores for 36 holes: Vardon, 157; Taylor, 161

YEAR	WINNER	VENUE	SCORE
1897	**Mr. H. H. Hilton, Royal Liverpool**	Hoylake	314
1898	**H. Vardon, Ganton**	Prestwick	307
1899	**H. Vardon, Ganton**	Sandwich	310
1900	**J. H. Taylor, Mid-Surrey**	St. Andrews	309
1901	**James Braid, Romford**	Muirfield	309
1902	**Alex Herd, Huddersfield**	Hoylake	307
1903	**H. Vardon, Totteridge**	Prestwick	300
1904	**Jack White, Sunningdale**	Sandwich	296
1905	**James Braid, Walton Heath**	St. Andrews	318
1906	**James Braid, Walton Heath**	Muirfield	300
1907	**Arnaud Massy, La Boulie**	Hoylake	312
1908	**James Braid, Walton Heath**	Prestwick	291
1909	**J. H. Taylor, Mid-Surrey**	Deal	295
1910	**James Braid, Walton Heath**	St. Andrews	299
1911	**Harry Vardon, Totteridge**	Sandwich	303
1912	**E. Ray, Oxhey**	Muirfield	295

YEAR	WINNER	VENUE	SCORE
1913	**J. H. Taylor, Mid-Surrey**	Hoylake	304
1914	**Harry Vardon, Totteridge**	Prestwick	306
1920	**George Duncan, Hanger Hill**	Deal	303
1921	**Jock Hutchison, Glenview, Chicago**	St. Andrews	296

After a tie with Mr. R. H. Wethered, Royal and Ancient. Replay scores: Jock Hutchison 150, Mr. R. H. Wethered 159

1922	**Walter Hagen, Detroit, U.S.A.**	Sandwich	300
1923	**A. G. Havers, Coombe Hill**	Troon	295
1924	**Walter Hagen, Detroit, U.S.A.**	Hoylake	301
1925	**Jim Barnes, U.S.A.**	Prestwick	300
1926	**Mr. R. T. Jones, U.S.A.**	Royal Lytham and St. Annes	291
1927	**Mr. R. T. Jones, U.S.A.**	St. Andrews	285
1928	**Walter Hagen, U.S.A.**	Sandwich	292
1929	**Walter Hagen, U.S.A.**	Muirfield	292
1930	**Mr. R. T. Jones, U.S.A.**	Hoylake	291
1931	**T. D. Armour, U.S.A.**	Carnoustie	296
1932	**G. Sarazen, U.S.A.**	Prince's, Sandwich	283
1933	**D. Shute, U.S.A.**	St. Andrews	292

After a tie with Craig Wood, U.S.A. Replay scores: D. Shute, 149, Craig Wood, 154

1934	**T. H. Cotton, Waterloo, Belgium**	Sandwich	283
1935	**A. Perry, Leatherhead**	Muirfield	283
1936	**A. H. Padgham, Sundridge Park**	Hoylake	287
1937	**T. H. Cotton, Ashridge**	Carnoustie	290
1938	**R. A. Whitcombe, Parkstone**	Sandwich	295
1939	**R. Burton, Sale**	St. Andrews	290
1946	**S. Snead, U.S.A.**	St. Andrews	290
1947	**Fred Daly, Balmoral**	Hoylake	293
1948	**T. H. Cotton, Royal Mid-Surrey**	Muirfield	284
1949	**A. D. Locke, South Africa**	Sandwich	283

After a tie with Harry Bradshaw, Kilcroney. Replay scores: Locke, 135; Bradshaw, 147

1950	**A. D. Locke, South Africa**	Troon	279
1951	**M. Faulkner, unattached**	Portrush	285
1952	**A. D. Locke, South Africa**	Royal Lytham and St. Annes	287
1953	**Ben Hogan, U.S.A.**	Carnoustie	282
1954	**P. W. Thomson, Australia**	Royal Birkdale	283
1955	**P. W. Thomson, Australia**	St. Andrews	281
1956	**P. W. Thomson, Australia**	Hoylake	286
1957	**A. D. Locke, South Africa**	St. Andrews	279
1958	**P. W. Thomson, Australia**	Royal Lytham and St. Annes	278

After a tie with D. C. Thomas, Sudbury. Replay scores: Thomson, 139; Thomas, 143

1959	**G. J. Player, South Africa**	Muirfield	284
1960	**K. D. G. Nagle, Australia**	St. Andrews	278
1961	**Arnold Palmer, U.S.A.**	Royal Birkdale	284
1962	**Arnold Palmer, U.S.A.**	Troon	276
1963	**R. J. Charles, New Zealand**	Royal Lytham and St. Annes	277

After a tie with Phil Rodgers, U.S.A. Replay scores: Charles, 140; Rodgers, 148

1964	**Tony Lema, U.S.A.**	St. Andrews	279
1965	**P. W. Thomson, Australia**	Royal Birkdale	285
1966	**J. Nicklaus, U.S.A.**	Muirfield	282
1967	**R. de Vicenzo, Argentina**	Holylake	278
1968	**G. J. Player, South Africa**	Carnoustie	289
1969	**A. Jacklin, Potters Bar**	Royal Lytham and St. Annes	280
1970	**J. Nicklaus, U.S.A.**	St. Andrews	283

After a tie with D. Sanders. Replay scores: Nicklaus, 72; Sanders, 73

1971	**L. Trevino, U.S.A.**	Royal Birkdale	278
1972	**L. Trevino, U.S.A.**	Muirfield	278

The American Open

YEAR	WINNER	VENUE	SCORE
1894	**Willie Dunn, Shinnecock Hills**	New York	Defeated Willie Campbell 2 holes
1895	**H. J. Rawlins, Newport**	Newport	173
1896	**J. Foulis, Chicago**	Southampton	173
1897	**J. Lloyd, Essex**	Wheaton, Ill.	162
1898	**Fred Herd, Chicago**	Shinnecock Hills	328
1899	**W. Smith, Chicago**	Baltimore	315
1900	**Harry Vardon, Ganton**	Wheaton, Ill.	313
1901	**W. Anderson, Pittsfield**	Myopia, Mass.	315
1902	**L. Auchterlonie, Glenview**	Garden City	305
1903	**W. Anderson, Apawamis**	Baltusrol	307
1904	**W. Anderson, Apawamis**	Glenview	304
1905	**W. Anderson, Apawamis**	Myopia	335
1906	**Alex. Smith, Nassau**	Onwentsia	291
1907	**Alex. Ross, Brae Burn**	Chestnut Hill, Pa.	302
1908	**Fred M'Leod, Midlothian**	Myopia, Mass.	322
1909	**Geo. Sargent, Hyde Manor**	Englewood, N.J.	290
1910	**Alex. Smith, Wykagyl**	Philadelphia	289
1911	**J. J. M'Dermott, Philadelphia**	Wheaton, Ill.	307
1912	**J. J. M'Dermott, Atlantic City**	Buffalo, N.Y.	294
1913	**Mr. F. Ouimet, Woodland**	Brookline, Mass.	304
1914	**Walter Hagen, Rochester**	Midlothian	297
1915	**Mr. J. D. Travers, Montclair**	Baltusrol	290
1916	**Mr. Charles Evans, Edgewater**	Minneapolis	286
1919	**Walter Hagen, Rochester**	Braeburn	301
1920	**E. Ray, Oxhey**	Inverness	295
1921	**Jim Barnes, Pelham**	Washington	289
1922	**G. Sarazen, Titusville**	Glencoe	288
1923	**Mr. R. T. Jones, Atlanta**	Inwood, L. I.	296
1924	**Cyril Walker, Englewood**	Oakland Hills	297
1925	**Wm. MacFarlane, Oak Ridge**	Worcester	291
1926	**Mr. R. T. Jones, Atlanta**	Scioto	293
1927	**T. D. Armour, Congressional**	Oakmont	301
1928	**J. Farrell, Quaker Ridge**	Olympia Fields	294
1929	**Mr. R. T. Jones, Atlanta**	Winged Foot, New York	294
1930	**Mr. R. T. Jones, Atlanta**	Interlachen	287
1931	**B. Burke, Round Hill**	Inverness	292
1932	**G. Sarazen, Lakeville**	Fresh Meadow	286
1933	**Mr. J. Goodman, Omaha**	North Shore	287
1934	**O. Dutra, Brentwood Heights**	Merion	293
1935	**S. Parks, South Hills**	Oakmont	299
1936	**T. Manero, Greensboro**	Springfield	282
1937	**R. Guidahi, Beverley Hills**	Oaklands Hills	281
1938	**R. Guldahl, Madison**	Cherry Hills	284
1939	**Byron Nelson, Reading, Pa.**	Philadelphia	284
1940	**W. Lawson Little**	Canterbury, Ohio	287
1941	**Craig Wood, Winged Foot**	Forth Worth, Texas	284
1946	**Lloyd Mangrum**	Canterbury	284
1947	**Lew Worsham, Oakmount**	St. Louis	282
1948	**Ben Hogan, Hershey, Pa.**	Los Angeles	276
1949	**Dr. Cary Middlecoff, Memphis**	Medinah, Ill.	286
1950	**Ben Hogan, Hershey, Pa.**	Merion, Pa.	287
1951	**Ben Hogan, Hershey, Pa.**	Oakland Hills, Mich.	287
1952	**Julius Boros, Southern Pines, N.C.**	Dallas, Texas	281
1953	**Ben Hogan, Hershey, Pa.**	Oakmont	283
1954	**Ed. Furgol, Clayton, Mo.**	Baltusrol	284
1955	**J. Fleck, Davenport, Iowa**	San Francisco	287
1956	**Dr. Cary Middlecoff, Dallas**	Rochester	281

The American Open – continued

YEAR	WINNER	VENUE	SCORE
1957	**Dick Mayer, Florida**	Inverness	282
1958	**Tommy Bolt, Paradise, Fla.**	Tulsa, Okla.	283
1959	**W. Casper, California**	Mamaroneck	282
1960	**Arnold Palmer, Latrobe, Pa.**	Denver, Col.	280
1961	**Gene Littler**	Birmingham, Mich.	281
1962	**J. W. Nicklaus**	Oakmount	283
1963	**Julius Boros**	Brookline, Mass.	293
1964	**Ken Venturi**	Washington	278
1965	**Gary Player, South Africa**	St. Louis	282
1966	**W. Casper, California**	San Francisco	278
1967	**J. W. Nicklaus**	Baltusrol	275
1968	**Lee Trevino**	Rochester	275
1969	**Orville Moody**	Houston, Texas	281
1970	**A. Jacklin, Britain**	Chaska, Minn.	281
1971	**L. Trevino**	Merion, Pa.	280
1972	**J. Nicklaus**	Pebble Beach, Calif.	290

American Masters

YEAR	WINNER	SCORE	YEAR	WINNER	SCORE
1934	**Horton Smith**	284	1955	**Cary Middlecoff**	279
1935	**Gene Sarazen**	282	1956	**Jack Burke, Jnr.**	289
1936	**Horton Smith**	285	1957	**Doug Ford**	283
1937	**Byron Nelson**	283	1958	**Arnold Palmer**	284
1938	**Henry Picard**	285	1959	**Art Wall, Jnr.**	284
1939	**Ralph Guldahl**	279	1960	**Arnold Palmer**	282
1940	**Jimmy Demaret**	280	1961	**Gary Player**	280
1941	**Craig Wood**	280	1962	**Arnold Palmer**	280
1942	**Byron Nelson**	280	1963	**Jack Nicklaus**	286
1946	**Herman Keiser**	282	1964	**Arnold Palmer**	276
1947	**Jimmy Demaret**	281	1965	**Jack Nicklaus**	271
1948	**Claude Harmon**	279	1966	**Jack Nicklaus**	288
1949	**Sam Snead**	282	1967	**Gay Brewer**	280
1950	**Jimmy Demaret**	283	1968	**Bob Goalby**	277
1951	**Ben Hogan**	280	1969	**George Archer**	281
1952	**Sam Snead**	286	1970	**Billy Casper**	279
1953	**Ben Hogan**	274	1971	**Charles Coody**	279
1954	**Sam Snead**	289	1972	**Jack Nicklaus**	286

American P.G.A.

YEAR	WINNER	RUNNER-UP	VENUE	SCORE
1916	James M. Barnes	Jock Hutchinson	Siwanoy C.C., Bronxville, N.Y.	1 up
1919	James M. Barnes	Fred McLeod	Engineers C.C., Roslyn, L.I., N.Y.	6 & 5
1920	Jock Hutchinson	J. Douglas Edgar	Flossmoor C.C., Flossmore, Ill.	1 up
1921	Walter Hagen	James M. Barnes	Inwood C.C., Far Rockaway, N.Y.	3 & 2
1922	Gene Sarazen	Emmet French	Oakmont C.C., Oakmont, Pa.	4 & 3
1923	Gene Sarazen	Walter Hagen	Pelham C.C., Pelham, N.Y.	1 up
1924	Walter Hagen	James M. Barnes	French Lick C.C., French Lick, Ind.	2 up
1925	Walter Hagen	William Mehlhorn	Olympia Fields, Olympia Fields, Ill.	6 & 5
1926	Walter Hagen	Leo Diegel	Salisbury G.C., Westbury, L.I., N.Y.	5 & 3
1927	Walter Hagen	Joe Turnesa	Cedar Crest C.C., Dallas, Texas	1 up
1928	Leo Diegel	Al Espinosa	Five Farms C.C., Baltimore, Md.	6 & 5
1929	Leo Diegel	Johnny Farrell	Hillcrest C.C., Los Angeles, Calif.	6 & 4
1930	Tommy Armour	Gene Sarazen	Fresh Meadows C.C., Flushing, N.Y.	1 up
1931	Tom Creavy	Denny Shute	Wannamoisett C.C., Rumford, R.I.	2 & 1
1932	Olin Dutra	Frank Walsh	Keller G.C., St. Paul, Minn.	4 & 3
1933	Gene Sarazen	Willie Goggin	Blue Mound C.C., Milwaukee, Wis.	5 & 4
1934	Paul Runyan	Craig Wood	Park C.C., Williamsville, N.Y.	1 up
1935	Johnny Revolta	Tommy Armour	Twin Hills C.C., Oklahoma City, Okla.	5 & 4
1936	Denny Shute	Jimmy Thomson	Pinehurst C.C., Pinehurst, N.C.	3 & 2
1937	Denny Shute	Harold McSpaden	Pittsburgh F.C., Aspinwall, Pa.	8 & 7
1938	Paul Runyan	Sam Snead	Shawnee C.C., Shawnee-on-Delaware, Pa.	8 & 7
1939	Henry Picard	Byron Nelson	Pomonok C.C., Flushing, L.I., N.Y.	1 up
1940	Byron Nelson	Sam Snead	Hershey C.C., Hershey, Pa.	1 up
1941	Vic Ghezzi	Byron Nelson	Cherry Hills C.C., Denver, Colo.	1 up
1942	Sam Snead	Jim Turnesa	Seaview C.C., Atlantic City, N.J.	2 & 1
1944	Bob Hamilton	Byron Nelson	Manito G. & C.C., Spokane, Wash.	1 up
1945	Byron Nelson	Sam Byrd	Morraine C.C., Dayton, Ohio	4 & 3
1946	Ben Hogan	Ed Oliver	Portland G.C., Portland, Ore.	6 & 4
1947	Jim Ferrier	Chick Harbert	Plum Hollow C.C., Detroit, Mich.	2 & 1
1948	Ben Hogan	Mike Turnesa	Norwood Hills C.C., St. Louis, Mo.	7 & 6
1949	Sam Snead	Johnny Palmer	Hermitage C.C., Richmond, Va.	3 & 2
1950	Chandler Harper	Henry Williams, Jnr.	Scioto C.C., Columbus, Ohio	4 & 3
1951	Sam Snead	Walter Burkemo	Oakmont C.C., Oakmont, Pa.	7 & 6
1952	Jim Turnesa	Chick Harbert	Big Spring C.C., Louisville, Ky.	1 up
1953	Walter Burkemo	Felice Torza	Birmingham C.C., Birmingham, Mich.	2 & 1
1954	Chick Harbert	Walter Burkemo	Keller G.C., St. Paul, Minn.	4 & 3
1955	Doug Ford	Cary Middlecoff	Meadowbrook C.C., Detroit, Mich.	4 & 3
1956	Jack Burke	Ted Kroll	Blue Hill C.C., Boston, Mass.	3 & 2
1957	Lionel Hebert	Dow Finsterwald	Miami Valley C.C., Dayton, Ohio	2 & 1
1958	Dow Finsterwald	Billy Casper	Llanerch C.C., Havertown, Pa.	276
1959	Bob Rosburg	Jerry Barber Doug Sanders	Minneapolis G.C., St. Louis Park, Minn.	277
1960	Jay Hebert	Jim Ferrier	Firestone C.C., Akron, Ohio	281
1961	Jerry Barber	Don January	Olympia Fields C.C., Olympia Fields, Ill.	277
1962	Gary Player	Bob Goalby	Aronomink G.C., Newtown Square, Pa.	278
1963	Jack Nicklaus	Dave Ragan, Jnr.	Dallas Athletic Club C.C., Dallas, Tex.	279
1964	Bobby Nichols	Jack Nicklaus Arnold Palmer	Columbus C.C., Columbus, Ohio	271
1965	Dave Marr	Billy Casper Jack Nicklaus	Laurel Valley C.C., Ligonier, Pa.	280
1966	Al Geiberger	Dudley Wysong	Firestone G. & C.C., Akron, Ohio	280
1967	Don January	Don Massengale	Columbine C.C., Littleton, Colo.	281
1968	Julius Boros	Bob Charles Arnold Palmer	Pecan Valley C.C., San Antonio, Tex.	281
1969	Ray Floyd	Gary Player	N.C.R. C.C., Dayton, Ohio	276
1970	Dave Stockton	Arnold Palmer Bob Murphy	Southern Hills C.C., Tulsa, Okla.	279
1971	Jack Nicklaus	Billy Casper	P.G.A. National G.C., Palm Beach Gardens, Fla.	281
1972	Gary Player	Tommy Aaron Jim Jamieson	Oakland Hills, Birmingham, Mich.	281

Piccadilly World Match Play

YEAR	WINNER	RUNNER-UP	VENUE	SCORE
1964	Arnold Palmer	N. C. Coles	Wentworth	2 and 1
1965	Gary Player	P. W. Thomson	Wentworth	3 and 2
1966	Gary Player	J. W. Nicklaus	Wentworth	6 and 4
1967	Arnold Palmer	P. W. Thomson	Wentworth	1 hole
1968	Gary Player	R. Charles	Wentworth	1 hole
1969	R. Charles	G. Littler	Wentworth	37th hole
1970	J. W. Nicklaus	L. Trevino	Wentworth	2 and 1
1971	Gary Player	J. W. Nicklaus	Wentworth	5 and 4

G. Player

A. Palmer

J. W. Nicklaus

R. Charles

Piccadilly World Match Play 1971

FIRST ROUND

Jack Nicklaus (U.S.) defeated Lu Liang Huan (N. China), 2 and 1

Nicklaus	Out:	435	534	544 – 37	In:	345	434	554 – 37	. . . 74
Lu Liang Huan	Out:	546	535	434 – 39	In:	244	524	455 – 35	. . . 74
Match even									
Nicklaus	Out:	444	534	334 – 34	In:	434	435	35	
Lu Liang Huan	Out:	544	534	443 – 36	In:	346	334	45	

Neil Coles (Great Britain) defeated Charles Coody (U.S.), 5 and 4

Coles	Out:	535	444	444 – 37	In:	344	423	445 – 33	. . . 70
Coody	Out:	446	444	434 – 37	In:	345	534	655 – 40	. . . 77
Coles 6 up									
Coles	Out:	344	434	545 – 36	In:	345	42		
Coody	Out:	435	433	445 – 35	In:	444	33		

Gary Player (South Africa) defeated Tony Jacklin (Great Britain), 4 and 3

Player	Out:	534	534	444 – 36	In:	354	334	465 – 37	. . . 73
Jacklin	Out:	526	434	444 – 36	In:	344	435	456 – 38	. . . 74
Match even									
Player	Out:	4w5	324	545 – X	In:	245	433		
Jacklin	Out:	5c5	434	535 – X	In:	444	434		

Bob Charles (New Zealand) defeated Arnold Palmer (U.S.), 1 up, 37 holes

Charles	Out:	534	434	444 – 35	In:	345	434	455 – 37	. . . 72
Palmer	Out:	445	434	434 – 35	In:	345	534	446 – 38	. . . 73
Charles 1 up									
Charles	Out:	435	433	444 – 34	In:	345	435	355 – 37	. . . 71
Palmer	Out:	435	424	444 – 34	In:	245	435	454 – 36	. . . 70
Match even									
37th hole: Charles 4, Palmer 5									

SECOND ROUND

Nicklaus defeated Coles, 7 and 5

Nicklaus	Out:	435	534	433 – 34	In:	344	534	434 – 34	. . . 68
Coles	Out:	544	424	544 – 36	In:	355	425	445 – 37	. . . 73
Nicklaus 5 up									
Nicklaus	Out:	424	444	454 – 35	In:	345	4		
Coles	Out:	435	533	355 – 36	In:	444	c		

Player defeated Charles, 2 and 1

Player	Out:	535	534	434 – 36	In:	344	334	444 – 33	. . . 69
Charles	Out:	435	535	444 – 37	In:	333	423	455 – 32	. . . 69
Match even									
Player	Out:	434	533	4c4 – X	In:	344	335	45	
Charles	Out:	545	433	445 – 37	In:	344	434	45	

FINAL

Player defeated Nicklaus, 5 and 4

Player	Out:	434	434	444 – 34	In:	345	244	444 – 34	. . . 68
Nicklaus	Out:	434	434	444 – 34	In:	344	335	344 – 33	. . . 67
Nicklaus 1 up									
Player	Out:	424	434	434 – 32	In:	3w5	43		
Nicklaus	Out:	535	534	444 – 37	In:	3c4	44		

Player received £8,500 ($20,400); Nicklaus £4,500 ($10,800); Coles, Charles £3,000 ($7,200); Lu Liang Huan, Coody, Jacklin, Palmer £1,500 ($3,600).

Ryder Cup Matches

1927   Worcester, Mass., U.S.A. June 3 and 4
Grand total: Great Britain 2 matches, U.S.A. 9 matches, 1 match halved

1929   Moortown, Leeds. April 26 and 27
Grand total: Great Britain 6 matches, U.S.A. 4 matches, 2 matches halved

1931   Scioto, Columbus, Ohio, U.S.A. June 26 and 27
Grand total: Great Britain 3 matches, U.S.A. 9 matches

1933   Southport and Ainsdale, Southport. June 26 and 27
Grand total: Great Britain 6 matches, U.S.A. 5 matches, 1 match halved

1935   Ridgewood, New Jersey, U.S.A. September 28 and 29
Grand total: Great Britain 2 matches, U.S.A. 8 matches, 2 matches halved

1937   Southport and Ainsdale, Southport. June 29 and 30
Grand total: Great Britain 3 matches, U.S.A. 7 matches, 2 matches halved

1947   Portland, Oregon, U.S.A. November 1 and 2
Grand total: Great Britain 1 match, U.S.A. 11 matches

1949   Ganton, Scarborough. September 16 and 17
Grand total: Great Britain 5 matches, U.S.A. 7 matches

1951   Pinehurst, N.C., U.S.A. November 2–4
Grand total: Great Britain 2 matches, U.S.A. 9 matches, 1 match halved

1953   Wentworth, Virginia Water. October 2 and 3
Grand total: Great Britain 5 matches, U.S.A. 6 matches, 1 match halved

1955   Thunderbird Golf and Country Club, California. November 5 and 6
Grand total: Great Britain 4 matches, U.S.A. 8 matches

1957   Lindrick Golf Club, Leeds, Yorkshire. October 4 and 5
Grand total: Great Britain 7 matches, U.S.A. 4 matches, 1 match halved

1959   Eldorado Country Club, California. November 6 and 7
Grand total: Great Britain 2 matches, U.S.A. 7 matches, 3 matches halved

1961   Royal Lytham and St. Annes. October 14 and 15
Grand total: Great Britain 9 matches, U.S.A. 14 matches, 1 match halved

1963   East Lake Country Club, Atlanta, Georgia. October 11–13
Grand total: Great Britain 9 matches, U.S.A. 23 matches

1965   Royal Birkdale, Southport, Lancashire. October 7–9
Grand total: Great Britain 12 matches, U.S.A. 19 matches, 1 match halved

1967   Champions Golf Club, Houston, Texas. October 20–22
Grand total: Great Britain 8 matches, U.S.A. 23 matches, 1 match halved

1969   Royal Birkdale, Southport, Lancashire. September 18–20
Grand total: Great Britain 16 matches, U.S.A. 16 matches

1971   Old Warson Country Club, St. Louis. September 16–18
Grand total: Great Britain 13 matches, U.S.A. 18 matches, 1 match halved

Walker Cup Matches

1922   National Links, Long Island. August 29
Grand total: Great Britain 4 matches, U.S.A. 8 matches

1923   St. Andrews. May 19
Grand total: Great Britain 5 matches, U.S.A. 6 matches, 1 match halved

1924   Garden City, New York. September 12 and 13
Grand total: Great Britain 3 matches, U.S.A. 9 matches

1926   St. Andrews. June 2 and 3
Grand total: Great Britain 5 matches, U.S.A. 6 matches, 1 match halved

1928   Chicago Golf Club, Wheaton, U.S.A. August 30 and 31
Grand total: Great Britain 1 match, U.S.A. 11 matches

1930   Royal St. George's Sandwich. May 15 and 16
Grand total: Great Britain 2 matches, U.S.A. 10 matches

1932   Brooklyn, Mass. September 1 and 2
Grand total: Great Britain 1 match, U.S.A. 8 matches, 3 matches halved

1934   St. Andrews. May 11 and 12
Grand total: Great Britain 2 matches, U.S.A. 9 matches, 1 match halved

1936   Pine Valley. September 2 and 3
Grand total: Great Britain 0 matches, U.S.A. 9 matches, 3 matches halved

1938   St. Andrews. June 3 and 4
Grand total: Great Britain 7 matches, U.S.A. 4 matches, 1 match halved

1947   St. Andrews. May 16 and 17
Grand total: Great Britain 4 matches, U.S.A. 8 matches

1949   Winged Foot, New York. August 19 and 20
Grand total: Great Britain 2 matches, U.S.A. 10 matches

1951   Royal Birkdale, Southport, Lancashire. May 11 and 12
Grand total: Great Britain 3 matches, U.S.A. 6 matches, 3 matches halved

1953   Marion, Mass. September 4 and 5
Grand total: Great Britain 3 matches, U.S.A. 9 matches

1955   St. Andrews. May 20 and 21
Grand total: Great Britain 2 matches, U.S.A. 10 matches

1957   Minikahda. September 1 and 2
Grand total: Great Britain 3 matches, U.S.A. 8 matches, 1 match halved

1959   Muirfield. May 15 and 16
Grand total: Great Britain 3 matches, U.S.A. 9 matches

1961   Seattle. September 1 and 2
Grand total: Great Britain 1 match, U.S.A. 11 matches

1963   Turnberry. May 24 and 25
Grand total: Great Britain 8 matches, U.S.A. 12 matches, 4 matches halved

1965   Baltimore, U.S.A. September 3 and 4
Grand total: Great Britain 11 matches, U.S.A. 11 matches, 2 matches halved

1967   Royal St. Georges, Sandwich. May 19 and 20
Grand total: Great Britain 7 matches, U.S.A. 13 matches, 4 matches halved

1969   Milwaukee, U.S.A. August 22 and 23
Grand total: Great Britain 8 matches, U.S.A. 10 matches, 6 matches halved

1971   St. Andrews. May 26 and 27
Grand total: Great Britain 13 matches, U.S.A. 11 matches

YEAR	WINNER	RUNNER-UP	VENUE	SCORE
1885	A. F. MacFie	H. G. Hutchinson	Hoylake	7 and 6
1886	H. G. Hutchinson	Henry Lamb	St. Andrews	7 and 6
1887	H. G. Hutchinson	John Ball	Hoylake	1 hole
1888	John Ball	J. E. Laidlay	Prestwick	5 and 4
1889	J. E. Laidlay	L. M. B. Melville	St. Andrews	2 and 1
1890	John Ball	J. E. Laidlay	Hoylake	4 and 3
1891	J. E. Laidlay	H. H. Hilton	St. Andrews	20th hole
1892	John Ball	H. H. Hilton	Sandwich	3 and 1
1893	Peter Anderson	J. E. Laidlay	Prestwick	1 hole
1894	John Ball	S. M. Fergusson	Hoylake	1 hole
1895	L. M. B. Melville	John Ball	St. Andrews	19th hole
1896*	F. G. Talt	H. H. Hilton	Sandwich	8 and 7

Thirty-six holes played on and after this date

YEAR	WINNER	RUNNER-UP	VENUE	SCORE
1897	A. J. T. Allan	James Robb	Muirfield	4 and 2
1898	F. G. Tait	S. M. Fergusson	Hoylake	7 and 5
1899	John Ball	F. G. Tait	Prestwick	37th hole
1900	H. H. Hilton	James Robb	Sandwich	8 and 7
1901	H. H. Hilton	J. L. Low	St. Andrews	1 hole
1902	C. Hutchings	S. H. Fry	Hoylake	1 hole
1903	R. Maxwell	H. G. Hutchinson	Muirfield	6 and 5
1904	W. J. Travis, U.S.A.	Ed. Blackwell	Sandwich	4 and 3
1905	A. G. Barry	Hon. O. Scott	Prestwick	3 and 2
1906	James Robb	C. C. Lingen	Hoylake	4 and 3
1907	John Ball	C. A. Palmer	St. Andrews	6 and 4
1908	E. A. Lassen	H. E. Taylor	Sandwich	7 and 6
1909	R. Maxwell	Capt. C. K. Hutchison	Muirfield	1 hole
1910	John Ball	C. Aylmer	Hoylake	10 and 9
1911	H. H. Hilton	E. A. Lassen	Prestwick	4 and 3
1912	John Ball	Abe Mitchell	Westward Ho!	38th hole
1913	H. H. Hilton	R. Harris	St. Andrews	6 and 5
1914	J. L. C. Jenkins	C. O. Hezlet	Sandwich	3 and 2
1920	C. J. H. Tolley	R. A. Gardner, U.S.A.	Muirfield	37th hole
1921	W. I. Hunter	A. J. Graham	Hoylake	12 and 11
1922	E. W. E. Holderness	J. Caven	Prestwick	1 hole
1923	R. H. Wethered	R. Harris	Deal	7 and 6
1924	E. W. E. Holderness	E. F. Storey	St. Andrews	3 and 2
1925	Robert Harris	K. F. Fradgley	Westward Ho!	13 and 12
1926	Jesse Sweetser, U.S.A.	A. F. Simpson	Muirfield	6 and 5
1927	Dr. W. Tweddell	D. E. Landale	Hoylake	7 and 6
1928	T. P. Perkins	R. H. Wethered	Prestwick	6 and 4
1929	C. J. H. Tolley	J. N. Smith	Sandwich	4 and 3
1930	R. T. Jones, U.S.A.	R. H. Wethered	St. Andrews	7 and 6
1931	Eric Martin Smith	J. De Forest	Westward Ho!	1 hole
1932	J. De Forest	E. W. Fiddian	Muirfield	3 and 1
1933	Hon. M. Scott	T. A. Bourn	Hoylake	4 and 3
1934	W. Lawson Little, U.S.A.	J. Wallace	Prestwick	14 and 13
1935	W. Lawson Little, U.S.A.	Dr. W. Tweddell	Royal Lytham and St. Annes	1 hole
1936	H. Thomson	J. Ferrier, Australia	St. Andrews	2 holes
1937	R. Sweeney, Jnr., U.S.A.	L. O. Munn	Sandwich	3 and 2
1938	C. R. Yates, U.S.A.	R. C. Ewing	Troon	3 and 2
1939	A. T. Kyle	A. A. Duncan	Hoylake	2 and 1
1946	J. Bruen	R. Sweeney, U.S.A.	Birkdale	4 and 3
1947	W. P. Turnesa, U.S.A.	R. D. Chapman, U.S.A.	Carnoustie	3 and 2
1948	F. R. Stranahan, U.S.A.	C. Stowe	Sandwich	5 and 4
1949	S. M. M'Cready	W. P. Turnesa, U.S.A.	Portmarnock	2 and 1
1950	F. R. Stranahan, U.S.A.	R. D. Chapman, U.S.A.	St. Andrews	8 and 6
1951	R. D. Chapman, U.S.A.	C. R. Coe, U.S.A.	Porthcawl	5 and 4
1952	E. H. Ward, U.S.A.	F. R. Stranahan, U.S.A.	Prestwick	6 and 5

1953	J. B. Carr	E. Harvie Ward, U.S.A.	Hoylake	2 holes
1954	D. W. Bachll, Australia	W. C. Campbell, U.S.A.	Muirfield	2 and 1
1955	J. W. Conrad, U.S.A.	A. Slater	Royal Lytham and St. Annes	3 and 2
1956*	J. C. Beharrell	L. G. Taylor	Troon	5 and 4
1957*	R. Reid Jack	H. B. Ridgley, U.S.A.	Formby	2 and 1

* In 1956 and 1957 the quarter-finals, semi-finals and final were played over 36 holes

| 1958* | J. B. Carr | A. Thirlwell | St. Andrews | 3 and 2 |

* In 1958, semi-finals and finals only were played over 36 holes

1959	D. R. Beman, U.S.A.	W. Hyndman, U.S.A.	Sandwich	3 and 2
1960	J. B. Carr	R. Cochran, U.S.A.	Portrush	8 and 7
1961	M. F. Bonallack	J. Walker	Turnberry	6 and 4
1962	R. D. Davies, U.S.A.	J. Povall	Hoylake	1 hole
1963	M. S. R. Lunt	J. G. Blackwell	St. Andrews	2 and 1
1964	Gordon J. Clark	M. S. R. Lunt	Ganton	39th hole
1965	M. F. Bonallack	C. A. Clark	Porthcawl	2 and 1
1966	R. E. Cole, S. Africa	R. D. B. M. Shade	Carnoustie (18 holes)	3 and 2
1967	R. B. Dickson, U.S.A.	R. J. Cerrudo, U.S.A.	Formby	2 and 1
1968	M. F. Bonallack	J. B. Carr	Troon	7 and 6
1969	M. F. Bonallack	W. Hyndman, U.S.A.	Hoylake	3 and 2
1970	M. F. Bonallack	W. Hyndman, U.S.A.	Newcastle Co. Down	8 and 7
1971	S. Melnyk, U.S.A.	J. Simmons, U.S.A.	Carnoustie	3 and 2
1972	T. Homer	A. Thirlwell	R. St. George's	5 and 3

American Amateur Championship

YEAR	WINNER	RUNNER-UP	VENUE	BY
1893	W. G. Lawrence	C. B. Macdonald	Newport, R.I.	4 and 3
1894	L. B. Stoddart	C. B. Macdonald	St. Andrews	5 and 4
1895	C. B. Macdonald	C. Sands	Newport, R.I.	12 and 11
1896	H. J. Whigham	J. G. Thorp	Shinnecock	8 and 3
1897	H. J. Whigham	W. R. Betts	Wheaton, Ill.	8 and 2
1898	Finlay S. Douglas	W. B. Smith	Morris County	5 and 7
1899	H. M. Harriman	F. S. Douglas	Onwentsia	3 and 6
1900	W. J. Travis	F. S. Douglas	Garden City	2 holes
1901	W. J. Travis	W. E. Egan	Atlantic City	5 and 4
1902	Louis N. James	E. M. Byers	Glen View	4 and 3
1903	W. J. Travis	E. M. Byers	Nassau	4 and 3
1904	H. Chandler Egan	F. Herreschoff	Baltusrol	8 and 6
1905	H. Chandler Egan	D. E. Sawyer	Wheaton, Ill.	6 and 5
1906	E. M. Byers	Geo. S. Lyon	Englewood	2 holes
1907	Jerome D. Travers	Arch. Graham	Cleveland	6 and 5
1908	Jerome D. Travers	Max H. Behr	Midlothian, Ill.	8 and 7
1909	R. Gardner	H. C. Egan	Wheaton, Ill.	4 and 4
1910	W. C. Fowness, Jnr.	W. K. Wood	Brookline	4 and 3
1911	H. H. Hilton	F. Herreschoff	Apawamis	37th hole
1912	Jerome D. Travers	Charles Evans	Wheaton, Ill.	7 and 6

YEAR	WINNER	RUNNER-UP	VENUE	BY
1913	**Jerome D. Travers**	**J. G. Anderson**	Garden City	6 and 4
1914	**F. Ouimet**	**J. D. Travers**	Ekwanok	6 and 5
1915	**R. A. Gardner**	**J. G. Anderson**	Detroit	5 and 4
1916	**Charles Evans**	**R. A. Gardner**	Merion	4 and 3
1919	**D. Heron**	**R. T. Jones**	Oakmont	5 and 4
1920	**C. Evans**	**F. Ouimet**	Engineers Club	5 and 4
1921	**J. Guildford**	**Robert Gardner**	St. Louis, Clayton	7 and 6
1922	**J. Sweetser**	**Charles Evans**	Brookline	3 and 2
1923	**Max Marston**	**Jesse Sweetser**	Flossmoor	38th hole
1924	**R. T. Jones, Jnr.**	**G. von Elm**	Merton	9 and 8
1925	**R. T. Jones, Jnr.**	**W. Gunn**	Oakmont	8 and 7
1926	**G. von Elm**	**R. T. Jones**	Baltusrol	2 and 1
1927	**R. T. Jones, Jnr.**	**C. Evans**	Minikahda	8 and 7
1928	**R. T. Jones, Jnr.**	**T. P. Perkins**	Brae Burn	10 and 9
1929	**H. R. Johnston**	**Dr. O. F. Willing**	Del Monte	4 and 3
1930	**R. T. Jones, Jnr.**	**E. V. Homans**	Merion	8 and 7
1931	**F. Ouimet**	**J. Westland**	Beverley	6 and 5
1932	**C. R. Somerville**	**J. Goodman**	Baltimore	2 and 1
1933	**G. T. Dunlap**	**M. R. Marston**	Kenwood	6 and 5
1934	**W. Lawson Little**	**D. Goldman**	Brookline	8 and 7
1935	**W. Lawson Little**	**W. Emery**	Cleveland	4 and 2
1936	**J. Fischer**	**J. M'Lean**	Garden City	87 hole
1937	**J. Goodman**	**R. Billows**	Portland	2 holes
1938	**W. P. Tarnesa**	**B. P. Abbott**	Oakmont	8 and 7
1939	**M. H. Ward**	**R. Billows**	Glenview	7 and 5
1940	**R. D. Chapman**	**W. B. McCullough**	Winged Foot	11 and 9
1941	**M. H. Ward**	**B. P. Abbott**	Omaha	4 and 3
1946	**S. E. Bishop**	**S. Quick**	Baltusrol	37th hole
1947	**R. H. Riegel**	**J. Dawson**	Pebble Beach	2 and 1
1948	**W. P. Turnesa**	**R. Billows**	Memphis	2 and 1
1949	**C. R. Coe**	**Rufus King**	Rochester	11 and 10
1950	**S. Urzetta**	**F. R. Stranahan**	Minneapolis	39th hole
1951	**W. J. Maxwell**	**J. Cagliardi**	Saucon Valley, Pa.	4 and 8
1952	**J. Westland**	**A. Mengert**	Seattle	3 and 2
1953	**G. Littler**	**D. Morey**	Oklahoma City	1 hole
1954	**A. Palmer**	**R. Sweeney**	Detroit	1 hole
1955	**E. Harvie Ward**	**W. Hyndman**	Richmond, Va.	9 and 8
1956	**E. Harvie Ward**	**C. Kocsis**	Lake Forest, Ill.	5 and 4
1957	**H. Robbins**	**Dr. F. Taylor**	Brookline	5 and 4
1958	**C. Coe**	**T. Aaron**	San Francisco	5 and 4
1959	**J. H. Nicklaus**	**C. R. Coe**	Broadmoor	1 hole
1960	**D. R. Beman**	**R. Gardner**	St. Louis, Miss.	6 and 4
1961	**J. H. Nicklaus**	**D. Wsong**	Pebble Beach	8 and 6
1962	**L. E. Harris, Jnr.**	**D. Gray**	Pinehurst	1 hole
1963	**D. R. Beman**	**D. Sikes**	Des Moines	2 and 1
1964	**W. Campbell**	**E. Tutwiler**	Canterbury, Ohio	1 hole
1965	**R. Murphy**	**R. Dickson**	Tulsa, Okla.	291
1966	**G. Cowan, Canada**	**D. R. Beman**	Ardmore, Penn.	285
1967	**R. Dickson**	**Marvin Giles**	Colorado	285
1968	**B. Fleisher**	**Marvin Giles**	Columbus	284
1969	**S. Melnyk**	**Marvin Giles**	Oakmont	286
1970	**L. Wadkins**	**T. Kite**	Portland	280
1971	**G. Cowan, Canada**	**E. Pierce**	Wilmington	280